Praise for

"I have worked with Andrew Faas for a number of years and what he advocates in *The Bully's Trap* is something he has effectively put into practice, particularly in building positive, high performance cultures."

—Glenn Murphy, Chair, CEO, Gap Inc.

"In this book *The Bully's Trap*, Andrew Faas takes bullying in the workplace as an issue that has long been relegated to human resources and powerfully and convincingly makes the assertion that this must be dealt with at the top."

—F. Ross Johnson, former CEO, RJR Nabisco

"*The Bully's Trap* provides an incredible insight on how corporate cultures influence behaviors. Andrew Faas is a voice of reason on this very real issue and this book should be required reading for anyone in management and included in the curriculum for business programs at colleges and universities."

—Paris Vlahovic
University of Toronto Graduate Rotman Commerce program, Specialist in Finance and Economics, graduated in 2012

"Andrew Faas in *The Bully's Trap* has really captured what goes on in the workplace. My regret is that I did not have the benefit of his guidance and advice when I was targeted—had I read the book then, I would have handled it in a better way which would have led to a better outcome."

—Catherine Labrosse,
Registered Nurse, Ontario, Canada

The Bully's Trap

The Bully's Trap

Bullying in the Workplace

ANDREW FAAS

TATE PUBLISHING
AND ENTERPRISES, LLC

The Bully's Trap
Copyright © 2013 by Andrew Faas. All rights reserved.

No part of this publication may be reproduced, stored in a retrieval system or transmitted in any way by any means, electronic, mechanical, photocopy, recording or otherwise without the prior permission of the author except as provided by USA copyright law.

In the stories I tell, some names and identifying details have been changed to protect the privacy of individuals and organizations.

The opinions expressed by the author are not necessarily those of Tate Publishing, LLC.

Published by Tate Publishing & Enterprises, LLC
127 E. Trade Center Terrace | Mustang, Oklahoma 73064 USA
1.888.361.9473 | www.tatepublishing.com

Tate Publishing is committed to excellence in the publishing industry. The company reflects the philosophy established by the founders, based on Psalm 68:11,
"The Lord gave the word and great was the company of those who published it."

Book design copyright © 2013 by Tate Publishing, LLC. All rights reserved.
Cover design by Rodrigo Adolfo
Interior design by Jake Muelle

Published in the United States of America

ISBN: 978-1-62563-855-7
1. Business & Economics / Business Ethics
2. Business & Economics / Business Etiquette
13.06.18

"The workplace is the most dangerous place to be in America."

—US Department of Justice (Grimme)

"Workplace bullying is kind of a new concept; it's like sexual harassment before Anita Hill...One of the biggest problems is that it is under the radar."

—Catherine Mattice (Petrecca 2010)

"Working in an environment that is free and safe of violence is a fundamental right—the fact is, all too many employees are being denied this right. These people deserve the highest level of protection."

—Andrew Faas

Dedication

This book is dedicated to Rollie

"No man can live with the terrible knowledge he is not needed."

—author unknown

Rollie, a magnificent, grey, regal Weimaraner with the saddest green eyes, was my constant companion during the time I was bullied and for the duration of writing this book.

Rollie was my first dog. I adopted him when he was a sixteen month old puppy, suffering from acute separation anguish, who as a result was the neediest dog I ever encountered. This was okay by me as he gave so much more than he needed. I soon discovered what it really meant to be needed and as he was dependent on me, I was dependent on him.

As a first time author I went through periods of writers block, self doubt to properly convey the messages and extreme frustration with the technology I was using (at one point over four thousand words evaporated into cyberspace!). Rollie was there with me through it all, and although he could not say the words, his eyes conveyed, "Don't worry Daddy—you can do it."

Much of what was written was thought through on my daily two to three hour walks with Rollie. He never tired of me talking (I think out loud).

Because I was bullied, for all too long a period I was depressed, angry and skeptical. Somehow like magic Rollie lifted all of this negative energy—just watching his butt and tail wag on our long walks, his joy when I came home, his constant need to be close and his unwavering trust in me, gave me such happiness. There is no question he helped me survive a horrific time, and in the process made me a better person.

On December 2, 2012, at seven years old, Rollie passed away in my arms—looking at me with those sad trusting eyes until I gently closed them.

Acknowledgments

I doubt that any book can be written in isolation. For those who try short change themselves and more importantly the reader. Writers need support, encouragement, and critical input. This I received in spades and am forever grateful.

My partner Lee Wells helped me through the periods of self doubt (there were many) and boosted my self confidence. Eleanor Pope who has been my Executive Assistant for fifteen years (which says something about both of us), has kept me focused, on track, and put some semblance of order in my scattered thoughts, sentences, and paragraphs (for those who know me, not an insignificant accomplishment).

Giving an author critical input is not an easy task, particularly if there is friendship involved—you want to be honest, but you also don't want to hurt feelings. Virginia Cirocco, Catherine Faas, Jennifer Grant, Karen Gruson, Velvet and John Haney, Ryan Jackson, Catherine Labrosse, Susan McClelland, Bobbi Reinholdt, and Paris Vlahovic, all gave me the much needed critical, direct feedback with such kindness it fostered even better relationships.

My associates at Iceberg Navigation, Richard Alderson, David Poirier, and Susan Shaw have given the book an added dimension with their contributing articles in the appendix.

The research provided by Glenn Pound in the early stages of the book helped me put the issue of bullying into context.

The professionalism and partnership with Tate Publishing made me appreciate the value of employees whose primary objective is to exceed the expectation of the customer. Today authors have many options, including self-publishing. As a first-time author, the experience was rewarding and Tate allowed me to focus on the content without having to spend a disproportionate amount of time dealing with the complexities of production and getting the book to market.

Finally to all of the people interviewed for this book, their stories raised my level of indignation on what all too many people have to endure every day, this has increased my passion and resolve to do what I can to stop bullying from occurring in the workplace.

Author's Note

If it had not been for Dr. Eli Canaani, an Israeli scientist who was funded by Israel Cancer Research Fund (ICRF), I would be dead today.

Eight years ago I was diagnosed with leukaemia. Thanks to a miracle drug called Gleevec, what was a fatal condition is now a chronic one. Also, this therapy is a forerunner to other therapies which target the cancer cells without harming the healthy ones.

Gleevec was developed as a result of twenty years of basic research by Dr. Cananni and his team.

Governments around the world and the pharmaceutical industry provide little investment in basic research. Without basic research there would be no discoveries, and without discoveries the chance for better therapies and cures is low.

ICRF was founded in 1975 and supports doctors and scientists who conduct basic research at all of the major research institutions in Israel.

I am a leading supporter of ICRF. To provide further support, twenty-five percent of my gross royalties realized from the sale of 'The Bully's Trap' and from speaking fees generated relating to the book will be directed to the Faas Foundation (www.faasfoundation.com), which in turn will be donated to ICRF.

Andrew Faas

Table of Contents

Introduction 19
Prologue 29

Part One — What's Culture Got to Do with It?

What's Culture Got to Do with It? 37
What Is Culture? 41
The Dictatorial Culture 43
    Case Study—From Canada's National Symbol To Canada's
    National Shame: The Royal Canadian Mounted Police
    (RCMP)—An Example Of A Dictatorial Culture 46
The Disjointed Culture 53
    The Catholic Church—An Example of a
    Disjointed Culture 54
The Stable Culture 55
    Case Study—On Becoming A Stable Culture—Shoppers
    Drug Mart (circa 1998–2008) 57
Organizational Leaders Don't Get It—Worse Yet
They Don't Want To Get It! 61
Bullying And Board Governance 67
Human Resources—Part of the Problem or Part of the
Solution? 71
    Case Study—Onto Pleasure Island—Pam's Story 78
    Case Study—Alone In a Man's World—Sonya's Story 84
Unions And Bullying 91
    Case Study—Who Does My Union Represent?—
    Patrick's Story 93

Part Two — The Dynamics of Bullying

What Exactly Is Bullying? 99
The Dynamics of Bullying 103
Making Distinctions. 111
Is There Gender Equality When It Comes To Bullying? . . . 119
Sexual Bullying. 121
    Case Study—The Ethic of Reciprocity—Linda's Story 124
Sexual Orientation and Bullying in the Workplace 129
    Case Study—No Way Out—Mark's Story 131
Hazing 139
Why Bullies Bully 145
    Case Study—They Wanted To Push Me Out—
        William's Story 151
    Case Study—Exploitation—Leila's Story. 157
Bullying and Stakeholders External To The Organization . . 163
    Case Study—Learning From the Parents—Toni's Story . . 164
    Case Study—The Customer Is Always Right—
        Allen's Story. 167
How Big Is the Issue? 169
Costs, Liabilities And Deadly Consequences 173
The Workplace As A Battlefield—Workplace Bullying and
    PTSD 179
    Case Study—A Father's Confession—Tim's Story. 181

Part Three — Effectively Dealing With The Issue

The Barriers 187
Bullying and the Attraction and Retention of Talent 191
Is There a Psychopath in the House? 197
    Case Study—I Flunked The Test And
        They Still Hired Me!—Andrew's story 198

Part Four — Guidance and Advice

Overcoming It—Advice to The Bullied 205
Defining the Unjust—Advice to the Bystander 215
Redemption—Advice to the Bully 223
Is Someone Close to You Being Bullied—
    Advice to Families And Friends. 227
A Happy Ending—John's Story 233
Employee Activists—Forcing a Cultural Transformation . . . 241

Appendices

Cyber-Bullying—High Tech Harassment 249
Conducting A Workplace Assessment Determining
    "At Risk" Position. 257
Bullying and Performance Management 263
Whistleblower Protection: Creeping Towards a Solution . . . 267
Index 291
Endnotes 303

Introduction

> "It is possible for a single individual to defy the whole might of an unjust empire to save his honour, his religion, his soul, and lay the foundation for that empire's fall or its regeneration."
>
> —Mahatma Gandhi

Bullying in the workplace is the biggest societal and economic issue we face. It is also the least understood, including how it is defined.

Many have asked—as you, the reader, should—"What makes you an expert on bullying in the workplace?" While I don't view myself as an expert, I do have extensive knowledge on the topic and firsthand experience.

My experience includes:

- over thirty years as a senior executive who has handled numerous bullying situations
- a background in labor relations and human resources
- early in my career being called out for being a bully
- being a bystander, witness, defender and resistor in numerous bullying situations
- having interviewed hundreds of people on the topic during the course of writing this book —and
- being retaliated against for being a whistleblower

Throughout my career I have coached numerous members of the gay and lesbian community on being discriminated against and bullied because of their sexual orientation. I have been fortunate in that, other than a few bigoted comments, I was not discriminated against or targeted as a result of my sexual orientation, but all too many of my friends and associates have been, and I hope that my support and coaching was helpful to them.

I have also mentored a number of women, helping them break through the "glass ceiling"—also cautioning them against the pressure to show their toughness by becoming bullies to get ahead.

To augment my experience and knowledge on the topic, extensive research was conducted.

Again, all of this does not necessarily make me an expert, but I think it qualifies me to make certain assertions, observations, viewpoints, guidance, advice and conclusions. More importantly through all of this, I have developed a passion to do what I can to bring the topic out from under the radar so that bullying is stopped and prevented.

My hope is that through this book, many will share my passion and, when appropriate, become employee activists to force the cultural transformations.

"Why do bullies bully?" The simple answer is because they can. Bullies bully because they work in an environment where it is allowed, condoned, encouraged, and even expected.

This is the basic premise of the book: where bullying is not allowed or condoned it will stop.

For bullying to stop, it requires much more than legislation or human resource policies and procedures, it requires a cultural transformation, and everyone has a role to play in this.

I assert that with these transformations, not only will the bullying stop, the performance of individuals and organizations will dramatically improve.

The issue of the bullying of children and adolescents in schools has received considerable exposure, largely due to the incidences of suicide where bullying is a factor. There is relatively little published material on workplace bullying that raises the level of awareness, discusses the impacts, and provides practical guidelines on how to effectively deal with and stop it. This then, is the goal of this book.

Also through this book, my desire is to increase the awareness of what constitutes bullying and the risks and the costs of bullying to the individual, the family unit, the organization, and the community.

The purpose of this book is not only to draw attention to what has become endemic in the workforce, but significantly propose solutions. Here I draw not only on my own considerable experience, but on the experience of others who have spoken to me in the course of writing this book.

In this book I challenge those who work in toxic cultures to become witnesses, defenders, and activist, never having to regret saying:

- I could have prevented the ruin of my coworker's career.
- I could have prevented the breakup of a family unit.
- I could have helped avoid the demise of an organization.
- I could have prevented a suicide or attempted suicide.
- I could have prevented someone going postal and killing others.

You will note that I have not focused much on rehabilitating the bully. Many believe that bullying is a learned behaviour and can be unlearned. This may be true, however I question the efficacy of stopping the bullying through conflict-resolution techniques, sending bullies to charm school, anger management programs, or diversity and sensitivity seminars. (These are usual methods human resource people employ when they are forced to deal with a bully).

While it is essential that organizations deal with bullying situations as they occur, it is important to understand that they are usually not an isolated situation and part of a cultural dynamic, so to prevent and eliminate bullying, I assert the following:

1. A fundamental shift in the attitudes of organizational leaders needs to take place where bullying is seen as not normal, natural, or necessary and must be effectively confronted.

2. Application of policies, procedures and programs on bullying needs to go beyond the rhetoric and the optics. Simply overlaying policies on a culture that condones abusive behavior is not sufficient.

3. Boards of Directors must monitor and audit cultural indicators.

4. If the CEO is the CBO (Chief Bullying Officer) the CEO must either change or be changed.

5. The fear factor needs to be eliminated in reporting wrongdoing.

6. The organizational response to bullying situations requires that the target and/or whistleblower do not become the villain.

7. Adoption of a performance management system that establishes clear and reasonable expectations and goals that does not pit employees against each other.

8. An employee index needs to become a major component on how managers are measured.

9. A "Red Flag" indicator system is required which shows warning signals where an employee could be a danger to himself or others.

10. Bullies need to be held accountable for verbal, physical, and/or psychological abuse of their targets.

11. Where workplace bullying is a factor in a suicide, the organization and the bully need to be legally accountable.

12. Where workplace bullying causes major harm to the target, the organization and the bully need to be held legally accountable.

Everyone Has A Story

"They wanted to force me out."

—common quote from people I interviewed

During the course of writing this book, almost everyone I spoke with about the topic had a story about their own experience or that of someone close to them (friend or family member). Close to 400 individuals were interviewed over a four year period. This reinforced for me the magnitude of the problem.

Throughout the book I use some of the stories I heard. These stories will put into context what I describe in the book, particularly organizational cultural dynamics and politics, the ways and means of bullying and the devastating impact that bullying can have.

The people I have worked with or interviewed are from across Canada and the United States, they represent a cross section of sectors, private and public, not for profit, governments, manufacturing, retail, health care, resources, transportation and financial services.

All of the interviews were unstructured, I just let them talk, relaying their experiences and those of their family member, friend, or coworker. Rarely did I have to interject to seek clarification. For almost everyone the experience is still fresh in their minds, because they keep reliving it. For many, to be able to talk about it brought some degree of closure.

In listening to their stories I tried to capture what people who are bullied go through under the following categories:

- Reason for being bullied
- Ways and means of bullying
- Reporting
- Organizational response
- Coping and/or reacting
- Impact on: physical and mental health, family, friends, employment
- Roles that bystanders play
- Post bullying outcomes

I do not claim this to be a scientific study, however, what I heard was consistent with research that had been done on the topic. The following outlines the dynamics and the impacts that were expressed.

- In 74 percent of the cases, the bullying was boss to subordinate.
- The main reason people were targeted was to force them out of the organization.
- Most of the targets got caught in what I refer to as "*The Bully's Trap*".
- Almost three quarters of the cases involved psychological bullying (which was often a mix of verbal and psychological combined), just over half were verbal harassment, and a few were physical.
- In over 66 percent of the cases threats were made, usually related to being let go or demoted.
- Just under half left the organization because of the bullying.

- Those who left had great difficulty in getting re-established.
- Just under a quarter would be considered sexual harassment, covered by statutes. More sexual, sexist, and gender discrimination was reported that did not rise to the level of legally defined sexual harassment.
- Almost all of the targets tried to deal with the situation alone, tended to make excuses for the bullying or blamed themselves, deny or minimize abuse as a way to survive it.
- All of the targets to varying degrees developed physical health problems.
- Over 60 percent of the targets reported symptoms consistent with Post Traumatic Stress Disorder (PTSD).
- Almost everyone described the experience as one of the worst they have ever encountered.
- Everyone indicated that the experience had a negative impact on their relationship with family members and close friends.
- In some cases, bullying was a factor in a marital breakdown.
- Almost a quarter considered suicide; there were a number of attempted suicides and a number of actual suicides.
- 60 percent described the CEO of their organization as "The CBO" (Chief Bullying Officer).
- A culture of fear existed in most of the organizations.
- Bullying was condoned in the majority of the organizations.
- Because of the culture of fear very few reported the bullying.
- In a few cases did bystanders become witnesses and defenders.
- Where the bystanders became witnesses and defenders, most were retaliated against.

- Bystanders became accomplices to the bully in over half of the cases.
- In the few cases where there was an investigation, there was an unsatisfactory outcome for the target.
- Just under half of the organizations had workplace violence/bullying/harassment policies and procedures in place. Most felt the policies, procedures, and programs were meaningless.
- Over 80 percent felt that Human Resources in their organizations was part of the problem.

∽

I want this book to make a difference, and I know it can. In June of 2011, I gave a convocation address where I talked about bullying. The following is an email that I received from a parent of one of the graduates.

> Andrew Faas:
>
> I am only hoping that this is the Andrew Faas that recently spoke at the graduating class on Saturday. If this is you I would like to tell you that your speech on that day impacted myself and my wife and family in a way that is hard to describe. You see the day before I had to quit my job of just over twenty-five years of service to a management bully who has only been there for just shy of two years. I tried to talk to the higher up management about this but was never taken seriously, they always sided with management. It's hard to say that I had to quit my job as I have never had to leave a job before. Your speech regarding the thought of what goes through people minds...people going postal is exactly what I have said and that it is harder not to go postal than it is. Also the thought about suicide in your speech impacted me, although I would never think about it but I'm sure many people do. I tried to find you

after the ceremony to tell you that you were my hero, I could not believe that this goes on every day and I only hope that it stops. Hearing your speech that day made me feel that I was not alone. Thank you, Andrew, for a speech that will stick with me for years to come.

Just a little note also to say that I start a new job where I'm sure that I will be happy on Monday.

—From a proud parent, graduating class 2011

Prologue

Bullying is all about power and control. Bullies are masters of deflection, who deceive and manipulate to achieve their end. Both organizations and individuals fall prey and in doing so usually become entrapped.

Throughout my career I have dealt with many bullying situations, in most cases effectively stopping the bullying. Also in a number of cases I, changed organizational cultures where bullying was tolerated and even encouraged. While I'm proud of this record, I can also recall situations where bullies convinced me into believing that the targets were the culprits.

Reflecting on those situations where I got sucked in (i.e. fell into the *Bully's Trap*) motivated me to help those who are/were targeted and as important, force change in organizational cultures where bullying is tolerated and encouraged.

The Bully's Trap: Vera's Story

In July of 2010, Vera was given an option to resign or be fired from her position as a marketing manager for an appliance manufacturer, a position she held for nine years. The reasons given for her termination were poor performance and insubordination. Not wanting to jeopardize her ability to relocate, she agreed to resign and received a modest severance.

Vera's last formal performance review was in February of 2009, where she received an "exceeds expectations" rating. In 2009, Vera received a merit increase which was above average, and incentive payout which recognized that she met all of her individual performance objectives. Over the previous eight years, Vera was rated and viewed as a high performer.

In August of 2009 as part of a restructuring, Vera's reporting relationship changed and Mark, who was also a marketing manager, became the director of the department and Vera's boss. Vera felt that she was more qualified than Mark, but recognized that he had more of a presence, which, in the culture of the organization, counted for more. While Vera was disappointed that she was not promoted, she indicated to Mark that she would support him.

When they were peers, Mark always viewed Vera as a threat. Anytime there was an opportunity to upstage her, he would, and he received credit for work that she had done. Vera's former boss recognized this and would always' tell her not to worry about it, that this was just part of Mark's aggressive nature, and that she would get credit for the contributions she made. Over the years, Vera and Mark were given equal exposure to senior executives to review marketing plans and major initiatives. Usually Vera would do most of the prep work and Mark would make the presentation. Vera was okay with this as she was not comfortable with public speaking. During the discussion periods, however, it was apparent that Vera was better prepared than Mark, a classic case of style over substance.

When Mark became the director, he started excluding Vera from the monthly marketing review meetings with senior management. Vera continued to prepare the presentations and the only feedback she got was when Mark could not answer a question, blaming Vera for not having prepped him well enough. Although for the subsequent meetings Vera added a number of notes for Mark to refer to, anticipating the questions he would be asked, Mark continued to have difficulty during the discussion periods. When the CEO suggested publicly that Vera should attend the meetings, Mark became concerned that if Vera attended these meetings, she would show him up and his position would be in jeopardy. Mark's resolution to this was to get rid of Vera.

Mark met with the vice president he reported to and Tim, the head of human resources, and indicated that he was dissatisfied with Vera's work, and he wanted to let her go. The vice president and head of human resources challenged Mark on the basis that Vera had always received a favorable performance review and the previous director thought very highly of her. Mark countered that the previous director covered up Vera's deficiencies, that he (Mark) carried most of the weight and Vera resented the fact that she was not promoted. He also insinuated that Vera and the previous director had more than a professional relationship. The head of human resources suggested to Mark that in order to fire Vera, he had to build a case.

From that point, Mark started to build the case. He kept important information from her, excluded her from meetings she needed to attend, gave her unrealistic targets and timelines and constantly badgered her. All of this started to have an impact on both her performance and attitude. When she challenged Mark on this, he would give her a written reprimand citing insubordination, sending copies to the vice president and Tim. Each time a mistake was made, a target or timeline not reached, Vera would receive a written warning, again with copies to the vice president and Tim. In addition to the written warnings, Vera was subject to verbal abuse, threats, and intimidation.

Knowing Mark the way she did, it crossed Vera's mind that she was being set up. Because Mark could prove that her performance was deteriorating, she started to blame herself for the position she was in. This made her more and more irritable, which caused more confrontations with Mark, which gave Mark more ammunition as he built the case.

Others in the department observed some of what was going on and most had their own challenges with Mark. Vera used to have a good working relationship with them; most would seek her help, which she readily gave. When it became apparent to them that she was targeted, everyone in the department shunned her and she was the subject of a lot of water cooler chats. Mark fed the gossip mill by telling people how badly Vera was handling the situation and that she "did not have her boyfriend there to protect her."

Because she was frustrated with the situation and herself, she often lashed out to others in the department. This put a strain on their relationships and was a factor in no one coming to her defense. Their rationalization was that they felt Vera was not handling the situation well and were upset with her attitude. Mark had some of them go to Tim to complain about Vera. Some only went because they were afraid not to, and others happily complied.

When Vera went to her doctor about some of the physical symptoms she was experiencing, the doctor strongly recommended that she go on disability because of the stress that she was under. Vera was told by Tim that the company would not pay disability benefits as they did not consider stress a disability. Tim told her that she was walking on thin ice and that if she went off on disability, it would be viewed as avoiding disciplinary action for performance and attitude and her absence would be without cause, which would result in her termination. Vera decided not to go on disability.

Vera, not knowing what to do next, complained to Tim that she felt that she was being bullied by Mark and was being set up to be fired. Tim defended Mark's actions and behaviors, indicating that the issues centered around Vera's performance and attitude and unless there was a significant improvement the company would have no choice but to terminate her employment. Tim suggested to Vera that a meeting be held to discuss the matter with Mark. Vera was not comfortable with this but felt she had no choice in the matter.

At the meeting, Tim told Mark that Vera had lodged a complaint about being bullied. Mark told Vera and Tim that he was not bullying, but only doing his job, correcting deficiencies and reacting when he felt that Vera was not being respectful. He went on to say that he was sorry that Vera felt the way she did, that he meant no harm. Tim offered that it was his view that this was more of a personality clash and that Mark's style may be a bit aggressive. Mark agreed with this assessment and promised Vera that he would work on his communication with her, adding, "I understand you are still upset with not getting the promotion, but for this to work you have to get over it."

On returning to the department, Mark followed Vera into her office, closed the door and said, "Now you really have gone too f—ing far! How dare you accuse me of bullying? You're the one who started all of this, you have never been any good and you never will be. Why don't you do everyone a favor and quit?" Vera burst into tears and slapped Mark across the face.

Mark picked up the phone, called Tim, and said, "I want you to fire that bitch right now. She just hit me."

Without getting Vera's side of the story, Tim gave Vera the option to be fired or resign.

The bullying did not stop here.

The advertising agency with whom the company had a long standing relationship, thought highly of Vera and offered to hire her, with the understanding that she would not be assigned any work related to her previous employer. When Mark was informed by the CEO of the agency of their intent, he reacted by saying, "If you hire her, you will lose this account." Vera was not hired and is still looking for employment. She has been blacklisted, and because it's a small world out there it will make it almost impossible for her to gain comparable employment in her field.

Part One

What's Culture Got to Do with It?

"It is not the prisoners who need reformation, it is the prisons."

—Oscar Wilde
1898—The Ballad of Reading Gaol

What's Culture Got to Do with It?

"Ordinary people, simply doing their jobs, without any particular hostility on their part can become agents in a terrible destructive process. Moreover, even when the destructive effects of their work become patently clear and they are asked to carry out actions incompatible with fundamental standards or morality, relatively few people have the resources needed to resist authority"

—Stanley Milgram
"The Perils of Obedience"

Bullies bully because they work in environments that allow, condone, encourage, and even expect it. They bully because they can. For the bullying to stop, a cultural transformation is required where bullying is not allowed— period!

Rarely a day goes by when there is not a story in the media about abuse of power, inappropriate behavior, corruption and greed on the part of leadership in every segment of our society, worldwide. Whether it is business, industry, government, education, social services or religion, none are immune.

Where this occurs in organizations, in most cases, there also exists a culture of fear, where bullying is condoned if not encouraged.

Reviewing recent examples of organizations who have gone down, or lost reputational value, the wrongdoing that led to the downfall could have been avoided if people within the organization who were in the know came forward and exposed the situation.

I assert that if there were not a culture of fear in those organizations that created the last financial meltdown, the meltdown could have been avoided.

AIG, Bear Stearns and Lehman Brothers are the good examples of cultures of fear, as well all three had CEOs who were also CBOs (Chief Bullying Officers.)

The Rise and Fall of Bear Stearns by Allen Greenberg is great reading for anyone in a leadership role. The book effectively describes how an organization went from having, what I describe below as a Stable culture to a Dictatorial culture, and the consequences of this shift. He also acknowledges that he had little patience for people complaining about the CEO, mistakenly believing that they were personality or style issues.

Allen Greenberg also acknowledges in the book that had he as Chair of the Board paid closer attention to the indicators of the cultural shift, he would have been able to have written a book more along the lines of *The Rise and Continued Rise of Bear Stearns*.

Reports that Ernst and Young, the long time auditors for Lehman Bothers were investigated for helping Lehman "cook the books" is an example of people who could have come forward early and did not.

The main reason that people do not come forward is a fear of retaliation. Consider what Sharron Watkins, the Enron Whistleblower, went through after she exposed the wrongdoing there (see case study in Appendix 4—"Whistleblower Protection: Creeping Towards a Solution").

Many organizations have put policies, procedures and whistleblower hot lines in place that provide a vehicle for people to report. The sad reality is people do not trust the mechanism, largely because they do not trust their leaders.

In December of 2010 Sheila Fraser, who was the Auditor General of Canada, issued a 375 page scathing report on the tenure of Canada's first Public Sector Integrity Commissioner, Christine Ouimet. This department is responsible for investigating complaints by public service employees of Government wrongdoing. From August 2007 to July 2009, 228 reports were filed. Of these only seven (yes seven!) were investigated, five were closed with no finding of wrongdoing and two remained under investigation!

Also in her investigation, the Auditor General found that Ms. Ouimet bullied her staff, where she "yelled, swore, marginalized and intimidated" certain PSIC employees and that she engaged in reprisal activities. Turnover of staff during Ms Ouimet's tenure was an astounding 50 percent for each of the two years.

Another example is that of Rupert Murdoch and the News of the World, Guardian News Services, in an article by Nick Davis on July 18, 2011, in the Guardian called "Sean Hoare knew how destructive the News of the World could be", tells how Hoare, now deceased, became a whistleblower when he broke the story that destroyed a 168 year old newspaper, and humiliated a media mogul. In explaining why he came forward he said "I want to right a wrong, lift the lid on it, the whole culture. I know, we all know, that the hacking and other stuff is endemic. Because there is so much intimidation in the newsroom, you have people being fired, breaking down in tears, hitting the bottle."

Research on workplace bullying has always detected serious organizational problems.

> "Crime is a logical extension of the sort of behaviours that is often considered perfectly respectable in legitimate business."
>
> —Robert Rice
> (former Attorney General)
> *The Business of Crime*

My own research illustrated the following problems that are evident in toxic cultures. Specifically:

- Leaders are more feared than respected by their employees.
- There is a disproportionate focus on the short term results, at the expense of sustainable long term, performance.
- Leaders are blind to massive risks.
- Leaders condone lax ethical standards.
- People are considered expendable.
- There is subjectivity and ambiguity in performance management and advancement.
- Fear is a substitute for motivation.
- There are few checks and balances.
- There is little transparency and disclosures.
- There is negligence at the governance level.
- Turfs and power are jealously guarded.

What Is Culture?

All too often, leaders view culture as something Human Resource people advocate to make people happy and or only relating to organizational values. This is a narrow view. Culture is all about hard core business issues. Culture is all encompassing. It is how an organization:

- is governed
- is led
- is aligned to values, beliefs, principles, purpose, vision and initiatives
- is structured
- communicates
- makes decisions
- assigns and aligns work
- operates
- measures performance
- holds accountability's
- rewards and recognizes
- hires people
- develops people
- advances people
- handles risk
- handles crisis

This section will describe and illustrate three types of cultures:

The Dictatorial
The Disjointed
and
The Stable

I encourage you to examine your workplace under these conceptual lenses. In doing this, it is important to note that these models are not categorical, they are more of a continuum to gain an understanding. You will find that your organization or department fits closer to one type, however the dominant ethos within your workplace culture will be the strongest indicator where your workplace fits on the continuum.

The Dictatorial Culture

In a Dictatorial culture it is all about hierarchy, power, and control. From the outside it appears to be a tightly knit unit—but this is only a facade. In this environment bullies are considered the heroes and individual is valued over team.

The characteristics of a Dictatorial culture:

- The boss has absolute authority, enforces order and always wins.
- Rigid enforcement of rules by means of actual threatened or imagined bullying/violence.
- The will and spirit of employees are attempted to be broken with fear and punishment.
- Humiliation is used extensively.
- There is extensive use of threats and bribes.
- There is a heavy reliance on unhealthy competition.
- Performance takes place in an atmosphere of fear.
- Rewards and recognition are highly conditional.
- People are taught what to think, not how to think.
- The boss does not get told what needs to be heard.
- People who "suck up" are favored.
- When things go wrong, employees are blamed and punished.

- Innovation, loyalty, good husbandry and good will are nonexistent.
- There is little to no transparency.
- There is an obsession with secrecy.
- Blind obedience is expected.
- Turfs are jealously guarded.

L Festinger in "A theory of Cognitive Dissonance" asserts that cultures can alter human behavior. The theory of cognitive dissonance is that people have a motivational drive to reduce dissonance. People do this by changing their attitudes, beliefs and actions. Dissonance is also reduced by justifying, blaming and denying. People can be highly impressionable and obedient when provided with a legitimized ideology and social and institutional support, especially when it is done through coercive means by an authority. The Stanford Prison Study and Millgram Experiment illustrate this.

Stanford Prison Study

The Stanford prison experiment was a study of the psychological effects of becoming a prisoner or prison guard conducted in 1971 by a team of researchers led by Psychology Professor Dr. Philip Zimbardo, PH.D., at Stanford University.

Twenty-four undergraduates were selected to play the roles of both guards and prisoners and live in a mock prison in the basement of the Stanford psychology building. Roles were assigned at random. The participants adapted to their roles well beyond what even Zimbardo himself expected.

The guards used authoritarian methods. Sanitary conditions declined rapidly when the guards refused to allow some prisoners to urinate or defecate and would not let the prisoners empty the sanitation bucket as punishment. Mattresses were a valued item in the prison, so the guards would punish prisoners by removing them, leaving them to sleep on concrete.

Some prisoners were forced to go nude as a method of degradation, and some were subjected to sexual humiliation, including simulated sodomy.

Five of the prisoners were upset enough by the process to quit the experiment early, and the entire experiment was abruptly stopped after six days.

Experimenters said that approximately one third of the guards exhibited genuine sadistic tendencies. Most of the guards were upset when the experiment concluded early. The prisoners also internalized their roles and grew increasingly passive and depressive.

The results of the experiment are said to support situational attribution of behavior rather than depositional attribution. In other words, it seemed the situation caused the participants' behavior, rather than anything inherent in their individual personalities. In this way, it is compatible with the results of the also famous Milgram experiment, in which ordinary people fulfilled orders to administer what appeared to be damaging electric shocks to a confederate of the experimenter.

The Milgram Experiment

The Milgram Experiment on obedience to authority was a series of psychology experiments conducted by Yale University psychologist Stanley Milgram, which measured the willingness of study participants to obey a figure of authority, who instructed them to perform acts that conflicted with their personal conscience.

The experiments began in July of 1961, three months after the start of the trial of German Nazi war criminal Adolf Eichmann in Jerusalem. Milgram devised his psychological study to answer the question: "Was there a mutual sense of mortality amongst those involved?" Milgram's testing suggested that it could have been that the millions of accomplices were merely following orders, despite violating their deepest moral beliefs.

Milgram summarized the experiment in his 1974 article, "The Perils of Obedience", writing:

"The legal and philosophic aspects of obedience are of enormous importance, but they say very little about how most people behave in concrete situations. I set up a simple experiment at Yale University to test how much pain an ordinary citizen would inflict on another person simply because he was ordered to by an experimental scientist. Stark authority was pitted against the subjects' (participants') strongest moral imperatives against hurting others, and, with the subjects' (participants') ears ringing with the screams of the targets, authority won more often than not. The extreme willingness of adults to go to any lengths on the command of an authority constitutes the chief finding of the study and the fact most urgently demanding explanation.

Ordinary people, simply doing their jobs, without any particular hostility on their part, can become agents in a terrible destructive process. Moreover, even when the destructive effects of their work become patently clear and they are asked to carry out actions incompatible with fundamental standards or morality, relatively few people have the resources needed to resist authority."

Case Study—From Canada's National Symbol To Canada's National Shame: The Royal Canadian Mounted Police (RCMP)— An Example Of A Dictatorial Culture

The image of a police officer on a horse in a scarlet coat and wide brimmed hat is Canada's most recognized symbol. Established in 1864, with headquarters in Saskatchewan, the Mounties evolved into a hugely complex police force with close to 30,000 employees.

Once an international icon of solid Canadian Values, the RCMP has found itself mired in a litany of organizational, legal and political controversies. In July 2010 the Canadian Broadcasting Service in a documentary called "Mounties Under Fire" described them as having a "broken culture."

The stated Core Values of the RCMP are:

"Recognizing the dedication of all employees, we will create and maintain an environment of individual safety, well-being and development. We are guided by:

- Integrity
- Honesty
- Professionalism
- Compassion
- Respect
- Accountability"

Based on a number of reports and surveys done, it appears that these values are nothing but propaganda, and that they are guided by the exact opposite of these.

When I look at the history and instances from 1978 to now, the RCMP stands out as an organization with serious organizational problems that has most of the characteristics of a Dictatorial culture. What really stands out are most are the denials, cover-ups and efforts to "keep it in the family."

The RCMP is structured on a paramilitary model which operates on a command and control hierarchy. Until 2006 they were allowed to operate with a high degree of autonomy and independence. The Government finally recognized that the wrong doings (which were getting a fair bit of media attention) could no longer be overlooked. A committee to investigate the allegations was established. Commissioner Giuliano Zaccerdelli appeared before the committee admitted he made mistakes and earlier gave the committee inaccurate testimony. He submitted his resignation to the Prime Minister the next day.

The departure of Zaccerdelli was not sufficient to change the culture. The RCMP is an insular organization, steeped in antiquated traditions which are counterproductive for a modern police force (or any other organization.) The culture of fear is maintained to cover up problems, preserve traditions, preserve the right of rank and resist change.

An internal RCMP report in 2010, entitled "RCMP Values-Driven Leadership" suggests that the workplace culture is badly in need of repair across the country and that bad management by some supervisors is "creating a toxic workplace, high levels of stress, and a culture of fear".

This report contains details about the use of sick leave. At the time of the report 336 employees in British Columbia alone were on long term disability with some having been on leave for up to seven years, and that health professionals estimate that 75 percent of those on sick leave are there for post traumatic stress disorder or "because of conflicts with supervisors and others within the organization".

In his book *Inside the Secret World of Ottawa and the RCMP*, Paul Palango describes the cult mentality that exists. A highly regarded former officer describes the culture this way, "The RCMP resists, any criticism, it does not respect the public, bureaucrats, or politicians. If one of the brass gets involved in a controversy, there is no will within the force to assess the persons culpability. The saying is, Respect the rank, not the story". The book also details where charges of abuse, assault, harassment and deceit were routinely made to disappear.

In 2009 the RCMP conducted a national survey to gauge morale, a process it undertakes every two years. The survey found that one in four employees in British Columbia had been "verbally harassed or tormented" within the past year. "Organizational culture" received the worst score of all, fifty-five questions and only 17 percent felt that the survey would make any difference. The survey also revealed that nearly 60 percent of RCMP employees have considered quitting their job in the past six months. Frustration, lack of recognition are the most common reasons, according to the survey.

In 2003 a scandal surrounding the administration of the force's pension and insurance plans, where there were allegations of fraud and abuse during the outsourcing of the plans. An independent investigator was appointed by the Federal Government. While the scandal was significant in and unto itself to taint the force, the review highlighted a fundamental flaw in the culture, rather than encouraging disclosure of wrongdoing, senior management retaliated against employees who brought the wrongdoings forward. In the investigators report titled "Restoring the Honour of the RCMP: December 2007" concluded "RCMP senior management allowed an unethical culture to develop, which discouraged the disclosing of wrong doing and did not hold individuals to account for unethical behavior." This committee commended the people who were viewed as whistleblowers by senior management, "as exemplifying the stated values of the RCMP, and those who subjected these people to reprisals expressed the exact opposite."

Professor Linda Duxbury of Carlton University in Ottawa conducted an extensive survey of RCMP members, which found extreme frustration with managers. "What they were frustrated with was the top down style of management, non supportive managers who don't trust or respect their members, manager's inability to communicate effectively with staff, politically driven agendas, managers who are perceived to be careerists who are governed by their personal agendas and managers who do not walk the talk."

In the September 2007 issue of Mcleans Canada, Sara Scott wrote an article called "Is this the end of the Toxic Boss? Judges are sending corporate bullies a message; treat your employees with respect." In the article she highlights the RCMP, citing the case of Officer Nancy Sulz, a $50,000 police officer with eight years experience who won nearly one million from the RCMP for being bullied by a senior officer.

*

The crisis within the RCMP hit a peak in July of 2010 when the Commissioner, William Elliot was accused of being a bully by ten deputy and assistant Commissioners who took their complaints directly to the Prime Minister's office. An unprecedented airing of dirty laundry for a notoriously insular organization.

Initially the Government decided to support Commissioner Elliot (the first civilian and first external Commissioner) because they recognized that he was trying to change the toxic culture, and agreed with Elliot's assertion that those who are against the changes are trying to force him out (a classic tactical move by bullies.) In the summer of 2011 the bullies won when Elliott decided to resign.

In November of 2011 Bob Paulson a lifelong Mountie who promised to conduct a review of outstanding complaints of harassment was appointed as the new Commissioner. In an article called "7 Issues facing the RCMP commissioner" by Laura Payton and Alison Crawford, CBC News, posted on October 27, 2011 cites "Culture" the sixth issue: "Mounties knew about it for years but it was only through the publication of Brown's report that the general public learned about the RCMP's so called penalty box culture where people who questioned authority were bullied, seconded to other government departments or sent on interminable French training."

*

It is now over a year since Paulson's appointment and he is now being challenged as "a man of words only" because he is failing to deliver on his commitment to positively change the culture where trust in the institution is regained.

The Disjointed Culture

The opposite of the Dictatorial is the Disjointed, one that lacks a firm structure, is highly emotional and reactionary. Best practice, state of the art employment policies are evident (usually plastered all over the place,) but in practice are non-existent. Usually departments and regional locations operate in silos. There are few checks and balances and bullies can and do operate freely. Here as in the Dictatorial bullies are usually considered high performers and heroes. Those who are bullied and the bystanders do not trust the systems in place to report abuse for fear of retaliation.

Characteristics of a Disjointed Culture:

- There is a lack of structure and discipline.
- Rules are not consistently applied.
- Events are reactionary.
- Rituals are substitutes for core values.
- There is a cover-up mentality.
- There is a lack of alignment to purpose, values, operating principles, vision and initiatives (Usually because there are none or there are too many.)
- Rewards and recognition are arbitrary, inconsistent and highly conditional.
- Cronyism & nepotism are evident.
- Emotions rule behaviors.

- Best practice, State of the art employment policies are evident but in practice nonexistent.
- Leaders live in false allusions.
- People are allowed to discredit others.
- Where there are multiple locations, it is a loose federation of companies operating in silos.
- Turfs are jealously guarded.
- There is little to no transparency.
- There is ambiguity and subjectivity in performance management.

The Catholic Church— An Example of a Disjointed Culture

John Thavis in his book *The Vatican Diaries* provides a behind the scenes look at the power, personalities, and politics at the heart of the Catholic Church. This book was published just before the resignation of Pope Benedict.

The Vatican that Pope Francis inherited has a culture that is disjointed and dysfunctional.

It is encouraging to witness the new Pope's recognition that the Catholic Church needs to restore its reputation of being respected defenders of human rights, peace, and social justice. To do this he must initiate a cultural transformation.

Although the initial words and actions are positive, it is yet to be seen whether Pope Francis can break the stronghold of the hierarchy and the various autonomous orders. Being the first Pope from the Jesuit Order is a significant indicator as the Jesuit's more closely resembles that of what I define as a stable culture—plus they have great resolve and discipline.

The Stable Culture

Stable cultures are highly disciplined, providing consistency, firmness and fairness in everything that occurs, which motivates and nurtures to enable individuals and teams reach their full potential.. They are not hierarchical, bureaucratic or violent. The Stable culture provides the consistency, firmness and fairness as well as a calm and peaceful structure that motivates and nurtures to enable the individuals and team to reach their full potential.

Characteristics of a Stable Culture:

- There is a governance model in place that monitors beyond the financials.
- There is a common and well understood vision and purpose.
- Values and operating principles are bed rocked as a foundation.
- Rules (a code of conduct and terms of engagement) are simply stated and consistently applied.
- There is an effective and inclusive strategic planning process that proportionately focuses more on sustainable long term performance and emphasises agility to respond to ever changing market conditions.
- All internal stakeholders are aligned to the vision, values, operating principles and the plan.

- Roles, responsibilities and accountability's are clearly defined.
- Vendor and Government relations are positive and fair.
- A four dimensional balanced score card measurement system is in place (customer, employee, financial and execution.)
- The four R's are rigorously followed, (doing the RIGHT things, the RIGHT way, by the RIGHT people at the RIGHT time.)
- Competency and co-operation are modeled and encouraged.
- Team is valued over individual.
- People are taught to think.
- People are motivated to be all they can be.
- People are measured more by the quality of their contributions than the quantity of output and time spent.
- There is a clear value exchange model in place (clear expectations of employees are set against what employees should expect from the organization to deliver on what the organization expects of them.)
- Bosses and subordinates have regularly, equal conversations, during which the boss asks things like "What do you need from me to deliver on what we have to achieve?"
- Leaders hear what they need to know.
- There is no fear of retaliation, and people are comfortable in bringing forward ideas, issues and opportunities.
- Courage is highly valued.
- Mistakes are considered learning opportunities.
- There is a high level of transparency.

Case Study—On Becoming A Stable Culture— Shoppers Drug Mart (circa 1998–2008)

It is not unusual to have subcultures within an organization, i.e.: where the overall culture is dictatorial or disjointed and some departments or locations having stable cultures, or conversely where the corporate culture is stable and some of the departments or locations have dictatorial or disjointed ones.

Having spent the bulk of my career in retail (twenty-three years with Loblaw Companies Ltd—Canada's largest food retailer—and ten years with Shoppers), overseeing in excess of one thousand locations, I have witnessed firsthand the dynamics of sub cultures and the resulting impact on performance. At Shoppers Drug Mart, Canada's largest drug store chain, where I was a management partner for ten years, we built a positive high performance culture— what I refer to as a "Stable Culture."

When we did the management led buyout (with KKR, Bain Capital, Charles Bank, DLJ and Ontario Teachers Pension Plan), we assessed that while overall performance was respectable, it was not performing to its full potential—the market was growing at a faster rate than we were—there where inconsistencies across the chain in staffing levels, store conditions, pricing, hours of operation, in stock positions, adherence to national programs—in essence the only consistency was inconsistency. To a great extent we were successful in the buyout because the other potential buyers could not see beyond the obvious problems and see what we did, which was a tremendous opportunity.

Unfortunately almost all of the senior management team had to be replaced—they had the technical capabilities, but as they fundamentally disagreed with the massive change that was required, we recognised early on that the prerequisite step was to have a team in place that bought into the plan. Most of the existing team were not on side as they felt their turf and base of power was at risk.

Glenn Murphy, someone I worked with at Loblaw's, was hired as Chair and CEO.

The new team we selected, with a few exceptions, were promoted from within. We chose well, as they became one of the most aligned, driven, and cohesive teams I have had the pleasure of working with.

Immediately following the buyout, we embarked on a program to totally transform the organization. The first step was conducting a cultural assessment of the corporate and regional offices followed by an assessment of all store locations.

Poor and marginal performing stores were benchmarked against comparable high performers. What we found was most of the high performing stores had the characteristics of a Stable culture and most of the poor and marginal performers had the characteristics of Dictatorial or Disjointed cultures. Bullying was evident in many of the corporate departments, the regional offices, and in the store locations which had the characteristics of Dictatorial and Disjointed cultures.

In tangible terms, we found the high performance stores had sustainable financial results, lower employment costs both in absolute dollars and as a percent of sales, higher customer satisfaction scores, lower staff attrition, higher sales per square foot, higher sales per transaction, higher in stock positions and higher inventory turns, and a higher sell through of seasonal items. We also heard directly from our customers, because of the inconsistencies in our offerings and their shopping experiences we were "over promising and under delivering."

To realize full potential we needed to significantly increase store count and operating hours, including additional 24 hour locations, extending hours and being open on Sundays and holidays.

A huge challenge was our reliance on pharmacists. Under legislation, drug stores cannot open, even for an hour, without a pharmacist on site. When we hired new pharmacists, it was like pouring water into a bucket with a big hole in the bottom. The attrition rate was over 30 percent and the vacancy run rate was just over 20 percent. To add to the dilemma, at the time, there was a worldwide shortage of pharmacists.

This alone was sufficient reason to go through a cultural transformation—ensuring all locations had a stable one. To reach our growth objectives we needed to become "Employer of Choice."

The transformation was complete within a year. It was hard work and we initially met with significant resistance at all levels. We cut through a lot of it by distinguishing what people disliked about the proposed changes, against what they disagreed with because they felt it was fundamentally wrong, making the point that "because you don't like or agree with something does not mean it is wrong—it may be different than what you would like or do, but is not necessarily wrong." By making this distinction and only debating what they fundamentally disagreed with vs. what they did not like, allowed us to move quickly. Many organizational transformations are derailed because of resistors who feel the changes will erode their autonomy or power.

Post our cultural transformation the variances in the performance indicators of the entire network of stores was dramatically reduced and the overall performance of the organization dramatically improved—specifically within five years the number of stores doubled, our EPS went from less than $1 to $2.64, the enterprise value went from $5 per share to $58 and we became the "employer of choice" the and attrition and vacancy rate for pharmacists went to low single digit—a well publicised Canadian success story.

✢

In 2008 both Glenn and I left Shoppers and a new CEO was hired. I will leave it to others to tell the post 2008 Shoppers story—other than to say, it is incredibly hard work to create a positive culture, but it is very easy to undo.

Organizational Leaders Don't Get It—Worse Yet They Don't Want To Get It!

The attitudes that organizational leaders have on bullying in the workplace is the single biggest determiner as to whether an organization is free and safe from bullying.

If leadership does not understand what constitutes bullying and are unaware of the consequences to the individual, organization and the community, bullying will be condoned and even encouraged.

If leadership believes that bullying is an effective tactic to achieve results, bullying will certainly be condoned and encouraged.

If the CEO is also the CBO (Chief Bullying Officer) bullying will not only be condoned and encouraged; managers throughout the organization will be expected to bully.

To understand the mindset of organizational leaders on bullying, I commissioned a group to interview 138 leaders—seventy-two CEOs, twenty-six Executive Directors, and forty Board Chairs across Canada and The United States. Of the 138, thirty-three were women.

These leaders represent a cross section of organizations, private and public, government, health care, manufacturing, financial services, retail, technology, transportation and resources. All but twenty-one of the organizations had multi locations and the number of employees ranged from a low of just under four hundred to a high of 64,000. Employees in sixteen of the organizations were represented by a union or an association.

The methodology I used was a structured but open-ended face to face discussion with each to gain qualitative insights. I do not claim this to be a scientific study, however the findings and observations validate and are consistent with the findings and observations on the interviews conducted with over 300 people who either have been bullied or had someone close to them that has been bullied (see Interviews Conducted).

With most of the leaders I interviewed there was a debate on what constituted bullying. Most would not accept the definition and viewed what I described as the ways and means of bullying as more of an aggressive management style. All did acknowledge however that sexual and racial harassment was wrong and should be considered bullying. These debates at the front end of the discussion helped put the overall discussions in context. While most felt my definition was too extreme, all but a few accepted it for the purpose of the discussion.

As the purpose was to gain an understanding on their attitudes and level of awareness, the interviews conducted avoided debating the rightness or wrongness of bullying.

The Findings:

1. The overall level of awareness and understanding of what constitutes bullying (and what does not,) is low. Most do not view bullying as workplace violence.

2. Although most want their organizations to be viewed as employers of choice and rate brand and reputation value as a high priority, few view bullying as a business risk in their organization.

3. The overall level of awareness and understanding of the impact that bullying has on the individual, organization and community is low.

4. When given our definition of bullying and the ways and means of bullying, all but seventeen indicated that they at some point in their careers have been targeted. Ironically many described their experiences and that of others they are close to, with great indignation.

5. 73 percent of the CEOs' indicated that they could argue, they were being bullied by their Board of Directors because of the pressure for short term results.

6. All but three of the Executive Directors of the not for profit organizations indicated that they spend a disproportionate amount of their time dealing with unreasonably difficult Board members.

7. 67 percent acknowledged that they use bullying as a tactic to get things done, improve productivity and or get better deals.

8. 69 percent believe that those who are targeted have performance or attitudinal issues, therefore, with the exception of sexual or racial bullying, it is warranted.

9. 71 percent condone bullying because they believe that fear is a better motivator than what they refer to as "that human resources stuff."

10. The notion that bullying causes targets to reduce their level of engagement, commitment and performance was widely rejected.

11. 52 percent of the leaders who operate where there is workplace violence and/or anti-bullying legislation were aware of the legislation and those who were aware felt that their organizations were compliant and only 7 percent could describe what compliant meant.

12. 86 percent indicated that they would not educate their employees on bullying because of a concern that employees

would use bullying as a sword or a shield when they are subject to disciplinary action.

13. While 62 percent indicated that they had stated values and operating principles only 14 percent of the sixty-two could recite what they were.

14. Only 27 percent could give adequate answers to cultural indicators (staff turnover (resignation rate) reasons people cite for leaving (absentee rate) number of people on stress leave—participation rate of engagement surveys—participation rate of people using EAP—history of human rights complaints).

15. Of the forty Board Chairs interviewed, six indicated their boards reviewed some of the cultural indicators.

16. 54 percent measure beyond the financials and 44 percent of this group uses a balanced scorecard methodology.

17. Of the thirty-four who had to deal with instances of bullying only four found the alleged bully to be at fault.

18. 69 percent considered staff turnover as a positive as it "gets rid of dead weight" and "allows for new blood."

19. 51 percent acknowledged that employees in their organizations may be afraid to report wrongdoings.

20. 86 percent felt that whistleblowers should be required to absolutely prove the allegation.

21. 52 percent consider whistleblowers treasonous.

22. 63 percent recognized that they may not be hearing what they need to hear.

23. 76 percent indicated that they often accept one sided representations when there is a conflict or disagreement.

24. 71 percent feel it is healthy to create a certain amount of conflict because "it makes people competitive."

25. 32 percent manage by "walking around."
26. 24 percent used the latest economic downturn to "clean house." Most of this group challenged their managers to force people out rather than lay them off.

Based on the work I have done in the area and my analysis of interviews conducted—it is my assessment that:

- Most organizational leaders don't get the issue—worse yet—they don't want to get it.
- Bullying is not considered to be an issue.
- More than half of the organizational leaders are bullies.
- Because of the pressure to deliver on short term results most organizational leaders condone and encourage bullying to force productivity and force people out.
- The attitudes that organizational leaders have on bullying, begets bullies throughout organizations. Bullies become the heroes and the bullied become not only the targets but also the villains (bullied bullies).
- As long as results are achieved, boards of directors are not interested in whether or not bullying goes on.
- Organizational leaders view fear as a more effective motivator than performance management systems.
- Workplace violence and anti-bullying legislation is viewed as an unnecessary aggravation that is relegated to either legal or human resources to fulfill the bare minimum.
- Short of a "going postal" situation, bullying will not be considered an issue with most organizational leaders.
- There is a fear that by raising the level of awareness on bullying, there will be abuse by employees, accusing managers of bullying when they try to correct deficiencies, and managers will become afraid to manage.

The recent scandal at Rutgers University illustrates the attitudes of organizational leadership on bullying.

In the fall of 2012 a video exposed Mike Rice, the Scarlet Kings men's basketball coach, verbally and physically abusing players. The President, Robert L. Barchi, was made aware of the video in November of 2012, but claims he did not view it. An ethics committee made up of board members and trustees did view it at a December 14 meeting and were satisfied that the three game suspension Rice received was adequate.

Barchi, in defending his role, placed blame on the athletic director, Tim Pernette, and other officials, saying they decided to follow a process involving university lawyers, human resource professionals, and outside counsel. This is based on a report that was commissioned that recommended that Rice be suspended and sent to an anger management course.

The fifty page report, conducted by an outside lawyer, made clear that Rice's outbursts "were not isolated" and that "he had a fierce temper, used homophobic and misogynistic slurs, kicked his players and threw basketballs at them." The report went on to describe him as "passionate, energetic and demanding" and that his behaviours constituted "permissible training" and he "caused them to play better during the team's basketball games."

After the video exploded in the media, Barchi had Rice fired. One can only assume the firing was in reaction to the disastrous publicity—not Rice's behaviour!

I assert if this case does not prompt leaders to view workplace bullying differently, nothing will.

Bullying And Board Governance

"Good governance does not just prevent misdeeds but actually improves the corporation."

—Ram Charan

How accountable are boards of directors for bullying that occurs in organizations they govern? As governance models continue to evolve, there is no clear answer. A better question is should boards be held accountable when bullying occurs and should they be responsible for ensuring that people in the organization are free and safe from bullying? I assert they should be. Bullying in the workplace exposes an organization to risk. As boards are responsible for protecting and growing enterprise value for the shareholder, anything that puts at risk the brand, and reputation value, puts at risk the enterprise value. Bullying puts an organization at great risk.

The scandalous frauds and abuses at Enron, WorldCom, Tyco and all too many others revealed gaping holes in the checks and balances that were intended to keep corporations honest and protect stakeholders, which resulted in the massive bankruptcies, cheated investors out of billions, caused massive layoffs and destroyed whole communities. Poor corporate governance has ruined companies; it destroyed a global accounting firm and threatened economies and governments. This has resulted in calls for board reform. For years directors have viewed that they are only responsible to the shareholder and have not factored in their owing a duty to other stakeholders-employees, suppliers, distributors, customer suppliers and any parties whose interests may be impacted by the organizations actions. For many that includes communities affected by local employment, environmental hazards or the exploitation of natural resources.

The primary role of a board is strategy formulation and policymaking; their accountability however is reduced when they do not consider that they are accountable for how the strategy and policies get implemented. This and the failures of oversight mechanisms expose directors to considerable litigation risk as they are the de facto the first and last defence for fiduciary responsibility. Whether it is boards being let down by management, or they are asleep at the switchboards, they must step-up and major reforms are essential.

Accountancy leaders from around the world met in Geneva in October of 2010 to discuss how to prevent a future financial crisis. The conference was hosted by the International Federation of Accountants (IFAC), and the United Nations Conference on Trade Development (UNCTAD).

Participants from more than fifty countries were on hand to address key questions including—What corporate governance reforms should be developed on a global basis? Three of their five key recommendations relate directly to board governance and indirectly to bullying in the workplace:

- "Boards should be focused on the long-term sustainability of their businesses. As such, corporate governance reform must include strengthening board oversight of management, positioning risk management as a key board responsibility, and encouraging remuneration practices that balance risk and long term (social, environmental, and economic) performance criteria."

- "Governance is more than having the right structures, regulation and principles in place— it is about ensuring that the right behaviors and processes are in place."

- "Governance mechanisms need to be strengthened at banks and other companies to ensure better oversight of risk management and executive compensation."

According to board governance guru, Ram Charan, in his books, *Owning Up and Boards That Deliver*, good governance does not just prevent misdeeds but actually improves the corporation.

Governance now means leadership, and gone are the days when board members would ceremoniously sit on boards, gathering prestige, and ensuring the company was in compliance with the rules and regulations of the industry. In pointing to the aim of progressive boards, Charan quotes Andy Grove, founder, former CEO and Chair of Intel: "[A progressive board aims] to ensure that the success of a company is longer lasting than any CEO's reign, than any market opportunity, than any product cycle."

In analyzing organizations that have had a reversal of fortune, and those who have gone down, a major factor was the profile of the CEO. The CEOs were also CBOs. Many have argued that there was no way to see the subprime mortgage crisis coming. We now know there were those that did, who blew the whistle, but were not heard because of CBOs who would not allow voices of dissent to be heard. CBOs see the organization as an extension of their own egos. This usually results in a hostile and toxic culture that costs companies dearly in lost productivity and intellectual capital, and has caused the downfall of many organizations. The question that must be asked here is where were the directors?

Lehman Brothers and AIG are two good examples of companies who could have survived and prospered if they had the benefit of better governance. On a much larger scale, the global financial meltdown could have been avoided had there been better governance.

Lehman Brothers was a storied institution that survived two world wars, the Great Depression, and practically every other calamity in its 158 year history, but was brought down in the largest bankruptcy by the their CEO Richard Fuld also known as "the Gorilla" because of his bullying. Many of his critics have blamed his bullying as the direct cause of Lehman's downfall. Fuld bullied everyone around him and created a culture of fear and intimidation to the extent that even the Lehman directors were afraid of him. The longest tenured CEO on Wall Street, Fuld kept his job as the subprime mortgage crisis took hold, while CEOs of the other institutions were forced to resign. The Lehman board remained reluctant to challenge Fuld as the firms share price spiralled lower and lower.

In his book, *A Colossal Failure of Common Sense*, insider Lawrence G. McDonald had this to say: "Richard had even turned Lehman's board of directors into a kind of largely irrelevant lower chamber. This was yet another group to rubber-stamp his decisions and collect generous fees. It was not for supplying well-meant and lucid wisdom in the current wild market-place, but for agreeing with the monarch, accepting his all-knowing take on the bank's investments. Above all, the board was not to rock the royal barge as it made its steady way down the stream."

One bad boss may be responsible for bringing AIG, the U.S. Economy, and the global financial system to their knees. Joe Cassano: The Man Who Crashed the World, as he was labeled by Michael Lewis in the August 2009 feature in Vanity Fair, or "Patient Zero of the Global Economic Meltdown" as nicknamed by Matt Tiabbi in Rolling Stone magazine, Cassano may be the world's poster boy CBO.

Cassano did become widely known as a bully across AIG, where the view of the boss was consistent, "a guy with a crude feel for financial risk, but a real talent for bullying people who doubted him. "AIG became a dictatorship" says one London trader. "Joe would bully people around. He'd humiliate them...." As in the case of Lehman Brothers, where was the board in all of this? Afraid and negligent.

Human Resources—Part of the Problem or Part of the Solution?

When I go into organizations to do a assessment, it is usually when the organization is in serious trouble or after a major incident. The first thing I attempt to determine is the role that human resources plays in influencing culture.

In many organizations and the many cases that I have dealt with, I have found that in well over 70 percent of the time human resources is part of the problem verses part of the solution.

In most cases human resource people view bullying as a personality clash or a management style issue and apply conflict resolution techniques to resolve the problem. Usually this makes the situation worse for the target and the bully feels further empowered because they have successfully defected their predatory behaviors, manipulating human resources to become their ally.

Organizational cultures dictate the role that human resources plays in preventing and stopping bullying.

In Disjointed cultures, human resources are called in after the fact and told to make the problem go away. Here the head of human resources is not a key player and lacks authority to hold bullies accountable. Where there is legislation, policies and procedures are put into place but not into practice. Targets and bystanders do not go to human resources because they know that human resources have no power and/or courage to properly intervene. Heads of human resources in these cultures are not equipped to deal with bullying. People working in human resources in these cultures know what bullying is because they are bullied and are cowered into thinking that this goes with the territory.

In Dictatorial cultures, human resources are also called in after the fact and told to make the problem go away. Here the head of human resources could be a key player and if so, is part of the problem. Bullies in these cultures are considered heroes, because they are viewed as high performers and have more credibility than their targets. Bullies know this and manipulate human resources to become their allies. Where there is legislation, policies and procedures are put into place but not into practice, compliance is for legal and security reasons verses prevention. Targets and bystanders do not go to human resources because they do not trust the leadership and by extension, people in human resources. Heads of human resources have the technical and academic credentials to be the best and the brightest in the profession but lack the influence and or courage to prevent and stop bullying from occurring. As in Disjointed cultures, human resource people working in these cultures know what bullying is, because they are bullied, and because of the environment in which they work, tend to become bullied bullies.

In Stable cultures, human resources are mandated to make employees free and safe from bullying. Here the head of human resources is a key player and has the authority not only to hold bullies accountable but more importantly prevent bullying from occurring. Legislation does not drive putting policies, procedures in place. They have been in place and are firmly entrenched and integrated in the way they conduct all of their affairs. Where there are instances, human resources conduct a swift but comprehensive investigation and resolve the situation. Targets and bystanders go to human resources because they trust both the system and the individual, and they are viewed as being neutral. Heads of human resources in these cultures are the best and the brightest of their profession because they apply their technical and academic background and experience and view their role as custodians of a positive culture. Human resource people working in these cultures know what bullying is because they have studied the topic.

While the CEO should own and drive the culture of an organization the head of human resources should be responsible and accountable for the integrity of the cultural health of the organization in the same way the CFO is responsible and accountable for the integrity of the financial systems and reporting.

The head of human resources is in the best position, regardless of the culture, to stop bullying from occurring. This should not be a matter of choice, it is a requirement of the job. If the head of human resources is not equipped or does not have the courage to make it stop, they are in the wrong position and as such, part of the problem.

The following outlines what human resources should do to ensure that the work environment is safe and free from bullying.

1. Conduct a comprehensive annual risk assessment.
2. Report findings and a plan of action to senior management and the board of directors for their endorsement and approval.
3. Develop and institutionalize policies, procedures and programs that address the issue of workplace violence.
4. Include workplace violence in the code of conduct.
5. As part of the hiring of and promotion to a management position process, have a psychological assessment be a condition of acceptance. No exemptions.
6. Develop a 'Terms of Engagement' agreement for all senior people to sign.

7. Ensure that the performance management systems are clear, fair, reasonable, not ambiguous or subjective thereby not giving a bully the opportunity to entrap a target.

8. Regularly train managers and supervisors on:

    - The policies, procedures and programs
    - Identification of risk behaviors
    - How to recognize, respond, report and prevent bullying

9. Conduct an annual awareness program for all employees outlining their rights and responsibilities on workplace violence.

10. Develop an incident investigation protocol that is swift, fair, objective, comprehensive, and minimizes the risk of the target becoming the villain.

11. In the event the CEO is also the CBO (Chief Bullying Officer), coach and guide him/her on changing their attitudes and behaviors. If they are not successful, they must report this to the Chair of the board of directors for their intervention.

Heads of human resources should view becoming part of the solution as a real opportunity to gain influence and relevance. Key to becoming part of the solution is to have credibility as an honest broker that acts in the best interest of all concerned.

The Red Flags

If bullying is occurring there are always indicators that it is happening. If people in human resources do not monitor these indicators they are part of the problem.

The majority of instances of bullying are not reported by either the target or the bystanders. Just because there are no reports or complaints of bullying, does not mean it is not going on. Usually bullying situations are talked about amongst employees and bullies build a reputation. If bullies are not confronted they are in essence allowed to run loose.

Other than employees talking amongst themselves, there are a number of other indicators that can identify and expose bullying and the bullies. To be part of the solution people in human resources need to follow up on any and every indicator. Where there is a bully running loose, there is almost always a number of telltale signs and by tying what may appear to be seemingly unrelated comments, events and situations together, it usually tells a story.

The following outlines the telltale signs that a bully or a number of bullies are running loose:

- The "noise level" or comments that people are making, direct and indirect. If there is a bully running loose, people will talk about it. People in human resources need to have people in the organization keeping them in the loop when they hear people talking about it. If the other indicators of bullying are there and the people in human resources are not hearing the 'noise level' they are out of the loop.

- Anonymous letters from people who are aware of a situation, but they are afraid to bring it forward.

- Calls to a whistleblower hot line. If there are no or few calls to the hot line, this is an indicator that there may be a fear factor in reporting wrongdoing.

- Comments made by employees on the social media e.g. blogs. Don't try to stop the Blogs or identify employees who post—stop the reasons employees feel it necessary to post.

- High turnover is an indicator that something is amiss, this connected with other indicators could expose bullying.

- Exit interviews, when people leave they should be asked whether bullying was a factor in their departure. People may not be direct in their comments, not wanting to burn bridges, but will usually give comments like, "He could be difficult to work with, or demanding, but we just learned to live with it." When comments like these are made, the interviewer should probe and make the person comfortable giving specifics.
- Increase in the absentee rate.
- Increase in the number of people on stress leave.
- Difficulty in getting people to transfer into a particular department or division.
- Engagement survey data comparison by department.
- Written comments that are made in engagement surveys. A lack of, or few written comments are an indicator that there could be a fear factor in expressing viewpoints or concerns.
- Comments made by vendors, recruiters and other service providers. While these people are external to the organization, they are often bystanders and may hear and see more of what is going on in an organization than what the organizational leaders and human resource people hear and see. These people could also be a bully's target.
- In organizations that have medical departments—regular and ongoing dialogue on levels of stress within the organization.
- Increase in calls made to the EAP (employee assistance program). The providers of these programs should be required to make human resources aware of bullying situations, with the assurance that the target's confidentiality is protected.

- Inconsistencies in representations made by a manager to discipline or terminate a subordinate. (A review of the subordinates performance history compared to what the manager is representing.)
- Managers who take all the credit when things go well and blame others when things go wrong.
- Individuals who constantly have disputes with others and are unwilling to compromise on their positions.
- Previous accusations or incidences of bullying.

On becoming aware of a situation or the probability of bullying occurring, the onus should be on human resources to check into it, immediately.

The first step is to review all indicators that are available which would add credence or discount the allegation or the probability of bullying. This is where it is important to tie the seemingly unrelated comments, events and situations together. As much of this information should be readily available, it should not take an inordinate amount of time to pull together. Depending on the situation, it may be necessary to conduct interviews with people who are close to the situation.

Armed with this information, the human resource person should meet with the suspected bully's immediate supervisor to review the situation and determine who should have a meeting with the suspected bully.

The purpose of the meeting is to outline to the person that bullying is suspected, along with the reasons for suspecting. If there is not a specific complaint and there is no direct evidence, the person should not be accused of being a bully, however, in the discussion it is appropriate to indicate that there are indicators that bullying is occurring and the organization is obliged to investigate and take the necessary steps to make sure that bullying is not occurring.

It is also appropriate to challenge the person on the reasons the indicators are there, for example asking why turnover is high. The ideal outcome is to have the person acknowledge that there is validity to the concerns being raised and agreeing to change the behavior. If this happens the person should be asked what the organization can do to help change the behavior, for example help with anger management. At the end of the meeting it must be pointed out that the expectation will be for the indicators to change, for example lower turnover and a much lower "noise level."

In situations where the person denies being a bully and rationalizes the indicators, then a more comprehensive investigation should be conducted. The person who is suspected of being a bully should be made aware of this and that people who are close to the investigation will be interviewed. It should also be made very clear that any intimidation or retaliation against people being interviewed will result in severe disciplinary action, up to and including discharge

The investigation should be swift, objective and comprehensive. If in the investigation bullying is validated, the bully must be dealt with. Part of the investigation should be an assessment as to whether the bully can be rehabilitated.

If the assessment concludes that the bully cannot change, the bully must be removed from the situation, where they are not able to bully others. If they are moved within the organization, it is important that this move is not seen to be a reward.

If the assessment concludes that the bully can change, the organization should offer to help put a corrective action plan in place and closely monitor the situation.

Case Study—Onto Pleasure Island—Pam's Story

In 2007, Pam was approached by an executive recruiter about an opportunity to join a global pharmaceutical company, Pam considered the executive recruiter to be a friend as they had worked for the same company a number of years earlier. The recruiter's recommendation that this opportunity would be a good fit for Pam was the sole reason why she considered the job.

At the time, Pam was a highly successful executive for another pharmaceutical company. In the ten years she worked for the company, she had been promoted six times. Prior to this, Pam spent six years as a top performer in the packaged goods industry, with a company she joined after graduating from university.

After the initial meeting with the executive recruiter, Pam met with the company's CEO, Karl, on a number of occasions, and Ellen the EVP of Human Resources. Pam had some reservations about taking the position, as she had heard from outside people that she trusted that the CEO was difficult to work for. Some even described him as a bully. Pam talked to the executive recruiter who assured her the rumours were not true.

Both the executive recruiter and Ellen assured Pam that while Karl was very direct, he was a fantastic leader, a visionary, very ethical and fostered a real team spirit.

Had Pam done more research before hiring she would have learned that Karl was, in addition to being the CEO, also the CBO (Chief Bullying Officer) and that the company had many of the characteristics of what I refer to as a "Dictatorial" culture. Pam's story highlights the importance of doing due diligence before deciding to change organizations.

Karl and Ellen were very aggressive in their pursuit of Pam. Karl, Pam later learned, had been overheard saying that he "nabbed a Trophy Hire" from a competitor.

Pam was offered a compensation package, which was significantly higher than what she was making and a guarantee of a promotion within the first year. These were clear indicators that she was a strategic hire and would be a contender to become Karl's replacement.

Based on what Pam felt was "a deal simply too good to pass up," she accepted the offer.

When Pam joined the company, her first priority was to meet with all the managers in her department. In these meetings most of the managers indicated that there were major cultural issues in the department and that the issues were linked to Nicole, one of Pam's direct reports. There were accusations that Nicole bullied people, both within the department and throughout the organization. The human resource representative for the department provided a background on Nichole and data that showed turnover in the department was high, largely due to Nicole's bullying. There was also an independent mediator's report, which characterised Nicole's leadership within the department like the movies *Mean Girls* and *Lord of the Flies*. Others in the company spoke about a long history of Nicole being constantly combative and pitting her team against others in the company. For some reason she seemed to have been able to do this with impunity.

Almost from the beginning, Pam found that she was being undermined by Nicole and being treated as if she had no authority. Nicole routinely refused to communicate directly with her, publicly refused to attend key meetings and walking out on meetings held by Pam. Pam also became aware that Nicole and Karl met on a regular basis without informing her. Nicole made it clear to Pam that she felt that she was more qualified than Pam to run the department.

In meetings with her peers, Pam learned that there was a lot of speculation that Karl and Nicole were having an affair, which was commonly known within the company and across the industry. The speculation gained some credibility with Pam when she, Karl and Nicole went on a field trip. Pam drove and Karl and Nicole ignored her the entire day. At the end of the day, Karl and Nicole went out for dinner without inviting Pam.

Pam went to Ellen for advice. Ellen went to great lengths to assure Pam that there was no merit in the speculation, that she had spoken to Karl about it and he acknowledged that he and Nicole had a strong working relationship, but it did not go beyond that. Ellen's advice was for Pam to meet with Nicole and confront her on the behavioral issues.

Pam met with Nicole who reacted badly and insisted that a meeting be held with her, Karl, Ellen and Pam.

Pam agreed with this and a meeting was held the next day.

At this meeting Karl and Ellen clearly wanted to appease Nicole, complimenting her on her performance and suggesting that her passion and dedication caused her to behave the way she did. Nicole agreed that this was the case, but did not mean to offend anyone and that while she was disappointed in not getting Pam's position, she wanted to support her nonetheless.

Pam wanted to reach an understanding that if Nicole was going to meet with the CEO, that she be made aware of it, and the CEO would not form a judgement or make a decision based on one-sided information. This was agreed. But Pam didn't feel relieved. She walked away from the meeting with her worst fears confirmed. Ellen and Karl were trying to pacify both Nicole and Pam. Nothing changed. Nicole continued to walk out of meetings with Pam, send her out-dated marketing reports to present at meetings, bullied Pam's employees and had private meetings with Karl.

Almost immediately after the meeting Karl started going after Pam with a litany of tactics designed to set her up for failure, including suggesting that Pam was leaking internal information to a competitor (which is what Karl did with a number of people he targeted as a rational to get them out.) Other tactics included leaving her out of key communications, making decisions in her area without informing her, leaving her out of key reports and emails to the management committee and continuing to deal directly with Nicole.

Pam now had no doubt that she was in trouble, but had no idea what to do. It seemed like a bad dream. Her life and career had been so on track just six months earlier. Remember Honest John and Gideon tempting the children away from school and onto Pleasure Island with promises of untold amusement and treats? But not a hint of what happened to the children there—Pam could relate.

Pam went to a number of peers for advice. While all of them were sympathetic, none wanted to get involved because they were afraid of Karl and none of them trusted Ellen. Pam learned that earlier in the year, five people went to the Board of Directors expressing ethical concerns they had about Karl, including their speculation about his affair with Nicole.

The situation was taking a serious toll on Pam's health. She was unable to sleep and began losing weight. The situation was so unreal and unjust that she constantly wondered if she had done something to deserve this. Pam had no one to confide in within the company. Her relationships with friends and family became increasingly strained. Pam finally sought professional help and was diagnosed with Post Traumatic Stress Disorder.

Pam then went for legal advice. The lawyer advised her to file for constructive dismissal, which she did, and negotiate a severance package. She left the company a broken woman, with no allies, including the executive recruiter, whom she firmly believes knew what Karl was like. The executive recruiter would no longer even return her calls.

The story does not end here. A few months later, Pam landed another position. She received a glowing six-month review with a comment on how well she fit into the workplace culture. A couple of weeks after the review her new CEO requested an introduction to Karl so that he could make a sales pitch. Pam facilitated the introduction. Less than twenty four hours after facilitating the introduction, the CEO fired Pam, saying she was a "poor fit." There was no question in Pam's mind that Karl discredited her to the CEO and Karl made doing business with them conditional on Pam being fired.

Fortunately, because Pam was highly regarded in the industry and had a solid track record prior to going to "Pleasure Island" she was able to relocate and is gainfully employed with an organization whose values are more in line with hers. While this is a happy ending for Pam it is unlikely that she will ever fully recover from the horrible experience and will always have to be concerned that Karl will seek further retaliation.

The Board of Directors did confront Karl on the issues brought forward by the five "Whistleblowers" and conducted a cursory (they did not even interview three individuals who could provide specific details on the allegations made—these names were suggested by the whistleblowers) investigation. They claim not to have found any wrongdoing. Karl adamantly denied the affair. Even after Karl was caught by a private investigator leaving Nichol's home after spending the night there and the evidence was given to the Board, they still did nothing. Keep in mind that this was in and around the same time frame that the Hewlett Packard Board fired their CEO because of the circumstances around an affair he was alleged to have had with a contract employee.

As time went on, Karl became even bolder in his questionable business practices and in his relationship with Nicole—he was, some suspected, taunting the board into firing him to trigger his golden parachute."

Four of the five whistleblowers were forced out of the company and found that they were under surveillance, phones and emails were being monitored before and after they left, and company funds were used for this activity. These people also found that they were "Blacklisted."

Thirteen months after the "cursory" investigation a key group of employee's staged a revolt—Karl abruptly resigned.

Author's Note

This case study captures the profile of a CBO—how human resources is culpable and part of the problem and the negligence on the part of the board.

During the course of my career, I have dealt with a large number of boss/subordinate affairs that created problems in the organization. One in particular stands out when a board member challenged me by stating, "This is common place. It's part of human nature." I expressed that I was offended that he thought I was that naïve and questioned,

1. "Is it okay for the CEO to breach company policy?"
2. "If he is breaching this policy, is it possible he is breaching other policies?"
3. "If the CEO is exempt from certain policies, how can they be enforced with others?"
4. "Is it okay for the subordinate to receive extreme favoritism because of the relationship?"
5. "Is it okay for the subordinate to abuse her power and bully others because of her access to the CEO?"
6. "Is it okay that the majority of management lost respect and confidence in the CEO?"

I indicated that as in most cases of this nature, "The affair is a secondary issue. It is what happens because of the affair."

Even with my retort, I don't think the board member got it!

Case Study—Alone In a Man's World— Sonya's Story

After graduating from university in 2004, Sonya enrolled in an elite firefighting academy and completed six months of rigorous training. Sonya was the only female in a class of thirty.

After graduating from the academy Sonya joined a fire department in a mid-sized Municipality. As in the academy, Sonya was the only female on the force. Initially, the relationship with her Captain and fellow Firefighters was positive.

By the time Sonya had two years in, she had come to know Rob, her Captain, quite well. Sonya was twenty-eight years old at the time and the Captain was fifty-seven. As a Firefighter, it is key to be a team player and because you are working in such close proximity for long periods of time developing close bonds is critical.

Sonya felt comfortable with Rob and viewed him not only as her superior, but also a mentor. Sonya knew that Rob had taken her under his wing and thought that his interest in her was strictly professional.

Over time Rob's attentions were starting to cross the line. He was giving Sonya a lot of special attention, singling her out for preferred assignments, always trying to sit next to her during meals, calling her on the intercom letting her know he was going to bed etc. The other firefighters started to notice what was going on and Rob's actions became the fodder for gossip and jokes.

While Rob's attentions were never overt or threatening, they were starting to make Sonya very uncomfortable. There was no question in Sonya's mind that Rob had a crush on her.

Sonya contemplated going to Rob and telling him his attentions were making her uncomfortable. However, she decided against this because she knew from what she had observed that Rob had a mean streak and retaliated against those who crossed him.

Sonya decided that her best option was to go to the Senior Captain and request a transfer to another station. While she did not file a formal complaint, Sonya did tell the Senior Caption the reason for her request. An immediate transfer was arranged.

A few weeks after the transfer Sonya ran into Ron when they were both off duty. In greeting Ron, Sonya was friendly but distant. Ron called her at home that night and demanded to know why she requested the transfer and why she was so distant with him. Sonya indicated to Ron that his call was totally inappropriate and he hung up on her.

The next time Sonya was scheduled to be on duty Sonya was told that Ron was in the Captain's office and wanted to meet with her. Sonya was frightened and refused to meet with him. While Sonya hid upstairs she overheard Ron go into a tirade with her Captain.

From that point, Ron mounted a campaign against Sonya. He was furious that she was rejecting and avoiding him. Although they worked at different locations and she worked for a different Captain, Ron still exercised considerable influence over her. In situations where all stations were called into a situation, (which is often the case) Sonya was under his command.

Using his cronies, Ron initiated a letter writing campaign. Through coercion he forced firefighters to write to the Senior Captain with fictitious concerns about Sonya's judgement and physical fitness, and that they considered her a safety risk. In addition to sending these "reports" to the Senior Captain, photo copies were widely circulated. When off duty Ron was constantly working the phones encouraging his cronies to find any reason to "write her up."

Sonya recalls a number of occasions she witnessed Ron speaking with her fellow firefighters, point in her direction, and walk away shaking his head.

The campaign was working, Sonya was being shunned by her fellow firefighters, they whispered amongst themselves, gave her sideways looks, and head shaking was routine. Almost no one would talk to her and she was excluded from most activities at the station, alone in a man's world!

Sonya also found that her equipment and gear were being tampered with. On one occasion, all of her gear and name tag were removed. When she found her overhead bag she found her name tag along with an open box cutter. Had Sonya just reached into her bag she could have seriously cut herself. Fortunately she was not hurt, but her sense of security was badly shaken. When Sonya reported this to her Captain, he accused her of setting it up to deflect from the concerns he and her fellow Firefighters had regarding her being viewed as a safety risk.

Sonya now felt that not only was her job at risk but also her personal safety. This was reinforced when she ran into Ron at her station and he threatened that something bad would happen if she stayed, and that by staying she was putting everyone she worked with at risk.

This was the breaking point for Sonya and in November of 2007 she made a formal complaint on the advice of a friend, who is a Lawyer.

Initially the complaint was filed with the Senior Captain, who referred it to an Assistant Deputy Chief who dealt with workplace harassment, discrimination and abuse issues. The advisor wrote up a report which went directly to the Chief who immediately forwarded it to the city's Director of Human Resources who initiated an investigation.

It was clear to Sonya at the outset that this was the first time that anything like this had occurred in the municipality. The union representing the firefighters initially resisted the investigation and needed to be educated on the legalities involved and the process. This resulted in a delay in getting the process started.

Almost everyone in the squad was interviewed. Most were clearly uncomfortable with it and made it known to Sonya that they did not like it. The fear factor was also at play and they knew that if it got back to Ron that they supported Sonya's claim, he was capable of retaliation. Sonya's isolation from her coworkers got worse, they resented a woman, junior Firefighter taking on a very senior Captain. Fortunately there were a few who supported Sonya's position, particularly those who had their own experiences with Ron.

Confidentially became an issue and it was very obvious to Sonya that there was a lot of talk going on. After people were interviewed they huddled amongst themselves to compare notes.

Sonya was interviewed a number of times during the process and often felt that she was fighting this alone against Ron, her coworkers, the union and to some extent the administration.

During the interviews the Investigator challenged whether Sonya was able to do the work of a Firefighter. The Director of Human Resources offered to move her to another Department. Through all of this Sonya remained resolved.

The investigation took a long three hundred and seventy nine days, over a year, to complete. During this period the isolation, fear and anxiety affected her health, requiring her to call in sick thirteen times. Sonya knew when she would not be able to perform as a firefighter, and if there was a fire when she felt this way, she would be a safety risk.

Finally the Investigator completed his report and found that her complaint had merit and the treatment she received, unjust. Included in the report were references to other situations where Ron bullied his subordinates.

By mutual agreement, Ron took early retirement.

Following the Investigators recommendations, all Departments in the city had a cultural assessment conducted and a number of positive changes were made to ensure that employees were not at risk of being bullied. Everyone went through an extensive awareness program on bullying and everyone in a supervisory position went through an extensive training program on bullying. The city is now considered a model for good leadership and staff relations. Also, there is a much more streamlined process to investigate complaints.

Sonya credits the Director of Human Resources for helping her cope through this long ordeal and keeping in touch with her to see how she was doing and also to assure her that the investigation was not forgotten. While the Director of Human

Resources should be credited for doing the right thing—the investigation took far too long—Sonya went through sheer hell for over a year—the length of time it took to conduct the investigation!

Author's Note

As indicated in the study, although the municipality and the director of human resources did the right things, next to the bullying the big issue here is the bureaucratic culture, where the time it took to resolve worsened an already bad situation. This has often been the case in situations I was brought into. When dealing with a bullying situation, it must be investigated promptly. Many human resource professionals become slaves to the bureaucracy and process becomes a substitute for purpose.

Unions And Bullying

In 1972 I began my career as a management labor relations officer in a Chrysler plant in Windsor Ontario, Canada. There I learned—by total immersion—conflict management. Mildly put, the environment was toxic, and barbarically tribal. Most of my time and energy was preventing fist fights between workers and foremen (pretty scary for a 140 lb twenty-three year old) and encouraging everyone in the plant from the supervisor to the janitor to be more delicate in their language.

My experience with unions also includes a ten-year stint as chief spokesman for Loblaw, Canada's largest retail food chain—which at the time was 90 percent unionized.

A few decades ago unions were necessary in protecting the rights and representing the interests of workers. It is safe to say that during the recent economic downturn, all too many employees have been and are exploited. Given this, it is perplexing that during this period union membership in the private sector has and continues to decline.

This is due, in part, to Right to Work legislation in some states, the most recent being Michigan. In part, it is reactions by management to organizing drives by bullying employees with the threat of closing or moving their operations, citing competitive factors. Also in part, it is because employees who are considered ring leaders in organizing drives being targeted by management.

In situations where I have been brought in to consult management on organizing drives, most executives' first instinct is to kill the drive at any cost. When I question why their employees feel it necessary to be represented, the reaction is usually, hostile silence.

There is no question that legislation and fear factor, are valid explanations for the reason unionized labor is on the decline.

Valid as they may be, there is a much bigger factor—which is how unions are viewed by workers—and the prevailing view is that unions bully their members into doing (or not doing) things that conflict with their interests, values and beliefs.

A recent example is in Ontario, Canada, where teachers were bullied into withdrawing from extracurricular activities as an act of protest because the legislated inability to strike—the withdrawal of the extracurricular was a form of "work to rule."

A large contingent of teachers did not support this action because it went against their professional philosophy. Notwithstanding their objections, most complied with the "work to rule' out of fear.

It takes a lot of courage to go against the union in situations like this because those who do will likely be viewed and treated as traitors forever by the die-hards and the union leaders.

Unions over the years have evolved to become social activists and major lobbying force which in many cases is for admirable causes. Some of this activism, however, is in conflict with the interests, values and beliefs of their members and union leaders have not responded well to the changing diversity of the membership and still are far too rigid in the whole concept that "if you are a brother or sister—there is solidarity."

Solidarity is important for any association or organization; however, when it becomes absolute and enforced through bullying it is no different than what I describe as a Dictatorial Culture.

Case Study—Who Does My Union Represent?—Patrick's Story

Patrick was a City Planner for a large North American City. He was one of twenty-six planners and they are represented by a Union for Municipal employees. Until he was discharged in 2010, Patrick had been with the city for fifteen years.

In July of 2009 the city approached the Union for concessions to help reduce a major deficit. The Union held a meeting with their members to review this. At the meeting Patrick indicated that the planning department was operating well under their capacity. This is something that Patrick has brought forward to his Manager on a number of occasions, usually when a planner left and when they were recruiting for a replacement. Patrick's view was that he and the other Planners could process double what they were doing. Every time he raised this with his Manager, Patrick was told that the work load was negotiated with the Union and to change this would be impossible. After the meeting, Doug, the Union Representative, asked him, "Are you crazy? *Never*, and I repeat, *never* raise this again!" Patrick fought back by indicating that the city was in trouble and needed to find ways to reduce costs and as a loyal employee he felt obligated to express his views. "In fact," he added, "I know in speaking with people in most departments, there are the same opportunities to reduce costs throughout the organization." Doug told Patrick it was not his place to offer solutions.

Patrick was disturbed by the reaction he got and decided to prove his point. Starting the next day he was able to process the daily assignments by noon, and requested additional assignments. Patrick's manager refused to do this, on the grounds that doing this would be in violation of the Collective Agreement.

Not being satisfied with this, Patrick went to the Director of Human Resources and was told the same thing, and was advised to "just leave it alone." Prior to this meeting, Patrick reviewed the

Collective Agreement and could find no reference to work load. When he challenged the Director on this, she indicated that it was an "unwritten understanding."

For two months, Patrick finished his assignments by noon, without exerting himself. During this period he constantly checked with his manager to have his work reviewed to make sure quality was not compromised. The manager indicated that she was satisfied with the quality of work.

Doug, the Union Representative was told by a coworker of Patrick's actions. Doug called Patrick and warned him that if he did not stop, his job would be at risk. Patrick responded by telling Doug that he was not doing anything wrong, in fact what he was doing was the right thing to do to help the city improve their finances. Patrick also made the argument that it was the Unions responsibility to find ways to help the city, thereby protecting jobs.

Almost every day after this, Patrick started to receive anonymous threatening emails, and calls to his home. The response from the Director of Human Resources to his complaint was, "I warned you; you brought this on yourself and there is nothing we can do to help you."

Concurrent with the threatening emails and calls, Patrick's Manager started to write Patrick up for poor quality work. At a disciplinary meeting Patrick produced a record of the times he asked his Manager to assess the quality of the work and each time he received a positive review. The Manager rationalized by indicating she had taken a closer look at the work. Doug also attended the meeting and advised Patrick that he had to support the Manager and if the quality of work did not improve, the Union would not be able to protect him. Patrick requested that an independent third party be brought in to assess his work. The request was denied. Patrick also requested that an investigation be done on the threatening emails and calls. This request was also denied and he was accused of being the instigator of the emails and calls.

Not one to give up, Patrick went to the police to report the emails and calls. An investigation was conducted, Doug and Patrick's coworkers were questioned. The investigation was inconclusive and Patrick was told that the only thing the Police could do is keep the file on record.

The emails, calls and poor reviews continued for the next few months. In January of 2010 Patrick was fired for poor performance, his salary and benefits were immediately terminated. The Union did not file a grievance.

In March Patrick suffered a major heart attack and went through a triple bypass operation. Now that he is recovering from this he is legally challenging the Union for failing to represent him and filing a civil wrongful dismissal case against the city.

Part Two

The Dynamics of Bullying

"There is exploitation when the Master considers the Worker not as an associate, as a helper, but as an instrument from which he must draw the greatest service at the lowest possible cost. The exploitation of man by man is slavery."

—Frederic Ozanam

What Exactly Is Bullying?

In the work that I have done on bullying in the workplace and the interviews conducted during the course of writing this book, I am amazed at the lack of understanding and awareness on the topic, as well as the myths and misinterpretations out there.

The Dignity at work Campaign in the UK defines workplace bullying as, "Persistent, offensive, abusive, intimidating, malicious or insulting behaviour, abuse of power or unfair penal sanctions, which makes the recipient fell upset, threatened, humiliated or vulnerable, which undermines their self confidence and which may cause them to suffer stress".

The Workplace Bullying Institute, founded by Drs. Gary and Ruth Namie, added to this definition: "Workplace Bullying is repeated, health harming mistreatment of one or more persons (the targets) by one or more perpetrators that takes one or more of the following forms:

- Verbal abuse
- Offensive conduct/behaviors (including nonverbal) which are threatening, humiliating, or intimidating
- Work interference—sabotage—which prevents "work from getting done."

Profile of a Bully

As we have recently witnessed with the Lance Armstrong debacle bullying is all about power, control, deceit, deflection discrediting, destruction and denial.

For over a decade Armstrong was considered to be 'The Boss" of the ICU—"The International Cycling Union" and he had total control over the doping culture of the US (Postal Service) team. In essence he was the Chief Bullying Officer of the sport.

Armstrong bullied to:

- force teammates to use the banned substances
- retaliate against those that took an anti-doping stance
- force out of the team those who did not comply
- force out of the team those who testified against him
- discredit those who went against him
- keep people in the know from exposing him
- influence the ICU

In a *60 Minutes* interview Scott Pelly asked the USADA CEO Travis Tigart what Armstrong could do to those who testified against him—Tigart's response was that Armstrong would "Incinerate" anyone that went against him. Tigart himself was bullied and received an anonymous death threat during the course of the investigation he was conducting.

Armstrong's behaviors, demeanor and comments made in various interviews, exposed him as a classic narcissistic bully. The Diagnostic and Statistical Manual of Mental Disorders IV classifies those who have a narcissistic disorder as "those who:

- are preoccupied with fantasies of unlimited success;
- believe that they are special and unique;
- require excessive admiration;
- possess a strong sense of entitlement;
- are inter personally exploitive and lack empathy;
- exhibit high levels of arrogance."

My experience in dealing with bullies—particularly those who have power—generally exhibit these narcissistic characteristics. Many are psycho paths and it may well be determined that Armstrong is one (see "Is There A Psychopath In The House?")

Like Armstrong, these people are have serious problems and they need to be stopped, hopefully through professional help they can change.

Bullying in the workplace is violence in the workplace. Most organizational leaders have difficulty in identifying it in those terms which I assert is the major reason that bullying is condoned and in many situations encouraged and in many organizations even expected of their managers.

The Dynamics of Bullying

David Beale and Helge Hoel in "Workplace bullying: Industrial Relations and the Challenge for Management in Britain and Sweden," reported that, "Very often, in 70 to 80 percent of the cases, the main culprit occupies a supervisory role while the target is a subordinate." This is consistent with research done in North America.

Coworkers also bully but they are usually bystanders who in many instances become complicit in the bullying.

The Dignity at Work Campaign in the UK offers the following as some of the most common ways that bullies torment their targets.

"Bullies may:

- Use terror tactics, open aggression, threats, shouting, abuse and obscenities towards their target.

- Subject their target to constant humiliation or ridicule, belittling their efforts, often in front of others.

- Subject their target to excessive supervision, monitoring everything they do and being excessively critical of minor things.

- Take credit for other peoples work but never take the blame when things go wrong.

- Overrides the person's authority.

- Remove whole areas of work responsibility from the person, reducing their job to routine tasks that are well below their skills and capabilities.

- Set for the person what they know to be impossible objectives, or constantly change the work remit without telling the person, and then criticize or reprimand the person for not meeting their demands.
- Ostracize and marginalize their target, dealing with a person only through a third party, excluding the person from discussions, decisions etc.
- Spread malicious rumours about the individual.
- Refuse reasonable requests for leave, training etc., or block a person's promotion."

Based on the many cases I have worked on, the following also could apply:

- Unreasonably delaying to approve or reject plans or objectives.
- Not providing constructive feedback.
- Making negative comments about the target to others.
- Dealing directly with the target's subordinates and ordering the subordinate not to disclose.

The Four Forms of Bullying

There are four kinds of bullying: verbal, psychological, physical, and cyber. While there are many similarities to bullying in schools, there are as many if not more differences—the main one being, bullying by children and pre-adults is far more overt whereas bullying in the workplace is far more calculated in the method by which the bully bullies.

In the workplace a combination of verbal, psychological and cyber bullying is more commonly applied—where in schools it is more of a combination of verbal, cyber and physical, or the threat of physical violence.

In schools bullies use cyber bullying to discredit or embarrass or "out" their targets, the same applies to the workplace, however it is more extensively used by the bully boss who does it under the guise of performance management.

My direct experience on being targeted was after exposing a corrupt executive. For well over a year I was subject to a combination of psychological, cyber, and (if you include a death threat as physical bullying) physical bullying in retaliation for blowing the whistle. My phones were tapped, my emails were hacked, I was called a "f—ing faggot" in a public forum and for a period of time put under surveillance. When I reported this, the board of directors chose to believe the executive and only when I produced documented evidence did they start to believe me.

Verbal Bullying

"People who are brutally honest get more satisfaction out of the brutality than the honesty."

—Richard J Needham

The most common form of bullying is verbal abuse, and includes taunting, badgering, belittling, racial and homophobic slurs, suggestive comments, gossip, and rumors. The bully usually rationalizes or defends the behaviors as "just kidding," or "I did not mean to offend, it is just my style," or "I lash out because of my passion," or "it's my way of getting people to produce more."

Psychological Bullying

"Calumny requires no proof. The throwing out of malicious imputations against any character leaves a stain which no after-refutation can wipe out. To create an unfavourable impression, it is not necessary that certain things should be true, but that they have been said."

—William Hazlitt

The most difficult to detect, psychological bullying is the systematic diminishment of an employee's sense of self through ignoring, isolating, excluding, setting up to fail, setting up to make a mistake (sabotage,) or shunning. Shunning—an act of omission, joined with rumour—an act of commission, is a forceful bullying tool. Both are unseen and hard to detect. The employee being talked about may not even hear the rumour but will suffer from its effects.

Psychological bullying can be used to alienate and reject a coworker or to purposefully ruin friendships. It can involve subtle gestures such as aggressive stares, rolling of the eyes, sighs, frowns, sneers, snickers, and hostile body language. Intentionally excluding an employee from a staff meeting or staff party is often overlooked as a form of bullying because it is not readily identifiable as name-calling or a fist in the face; the results are not as obvious as a black eye or a damaged computer program; and the pain it causes is usually hidden or when expressed, dismissed ("You didn't miss much of a meeting anyway; nothing important happened"). For the bullied, psychological bullying is very difficult to defend against. It is usually a combination of a number of things at play, and that is why it is so important for the target to be on alert for what seems to be out of the norm, tying seemingly unrelated comments, situations and events together.

Physical Bullying

"Violence is, essentially, a confession of ultimate inarticulateness."

—Time Magazine

In the workplace physical bullying is less common than in schools. However if you include the threat of physical violence it becomes more common. It is more common in blue collar environments than in the office.

There are two professions where there has been a decrease of an already low rate of horizontal physical violence, i.e. violence against a worker by a coworker, and a significant increase in vertical physical violence, i.e. violence by someone under their care: nursing and education. Both of these groups do have incidences of horizontal and vertical verbal and psychological bullying, but the biggest concern expressed by both—and the most wearing—has been the physical attacks by people they are trying to help—patients and students.

The same day that a group of young girls from Carson City, Nevada were arrested for inviting on Facebook other middle school students to join them in "Attack a Teacher Day," a seventeen-year-old boy in Omaha, Nebraska shot and killed his assistant principal and seriously wounded his vice principal before killing himself. The girls were considered good students who had good grades and some held leadership positions in their middle school, a.k.a. high status social bullies. The boy had been recently suspended from high school.

In her article "Violence: Not in My Job Description," Laura A. Stokowski, RN, MS, discussed the prevalence of violence against nurses in the workplace (48 percent of all non-fatal injuries from occupational assaults and violence occurred in health care and social service settings), and the reasons nurses often do not report the abuse:

> "Nurses may fear reporting violence will affect patient satisfaction scores, or that hospital administrators will retaliate. Some don't know the hospital's reporting policy or believe that they can only report visible physical injuries. Other nurses avoid reporting violence because they believe that supervisors will question their competence, suspect that they somehow provoked the incident, or label them as troublemakers if they have no obvious physical injury.

When nurses do report incidents of abuse, more than 85 percent do so only verbally."

In "Nurses' Experience of Violence in Alberta and British Columbia Hospitals," researchers SM Duncan, K. Hyndman, CA Estabrooks, et al. found that 46 percent of nurses experienced one or more types of verbal, psychological, or physical violence in the past five shifts they worked.

Hazing (which I have expanded on in this section) is a form of physical bullying which does not receive the exposure it should. Being the target of this type of aggression is perhaps the most humiliating experience that one can face in the workplace and is in all too many workplaces considered harmless fun.

Cyber Bullying

In today's world cyber bullying has grown to the extent that it is now considered to be a major category of bullying. I assert that most bullies are cowards and the technologies have given many the opportunities to be brave. In Appendix 1, you will see an article called Cyber Bullying—High Tech Harassment, which provides a current perspective on the topic and methods by which it can be dealt with.

The Dynamics of Bullying At Play

As you have seen in Vera's story and will see in the other stories—bullies are masters of deflection who usually discredit their targets to the point the target becomes the villain—they usually (in what Stanford Engineering School Management Professor and *Good Boss, Bad Boss* author Robert Sutton has labelled) "kiss up and kick down"—and because they are seen as high producers they are viewed as the hero's who garner more credibility than the target.

Part One deals with the organizational dynamics of bullying and as you will see in the case studies, the following organizational characteristics are at play:

- A dictatorial or a disjointed culture
- A culture that rewards the bully and blames the bullied
- Practices that encourages individualism more than team
- A culture where power is vested without checks and balances.

Also in the stories you will see a pattern that is usually evident in bullying:

- A triggering event which is usually a comment, criticism, challenge or action that the bully takes exception to. The trigger could also be the bully viewing the target as a threat.
- The bullies resolve to punish the target.
- The bullies actions
- The bystanders become complicit.
- The target falls into the bullies trap.
- If caught the bullies deflection by turning the target into the culprit.
- The target is reprimanded or gets fired or quits.
- The bully identifies the next target.
- In all too few instances bystanders become witnesses and defenders.
- In even rarer instances the targets take steps to challenge the bully.

Making Distinctions

> A point of view can be a dangerous luxury when substituted for insight and understanding.
>
> —Marshall Mcluhan,
> The Gutenberg Galaxy

Although bullying is the focus of this book, it is critical to understand what bullying is not. The distinctions may not be obvious at first glance and can hide behind myths and misinterpretations. Just as failing to recognize an act of bullying and labeling it as a conflict or rationalizing it as a joke, overextending terms, and labeling behaviors discredit efforts to properly deal with bullying.

Disagreements and conflict is a normal dynamic that occurs in all environments. It would be wrong to label all disagreements and conflicts as bullying. It is healthy to raise and debate differing views, as long as it is done in an open, honest, and direct way, and resolved—even if the resolution is to "agree to disagree." Not only is it healthy to have these debates—I assert it is essential to bring differences out in the open, rather than have them fester.

When disagreements or opposing viewpoints are stifled or the parties involved are constantly battling, bullying is likely at play.

Some bullying activities are also criminal offenses. They could be hate crimes against an employees race, religion, real or perceived sexual orientation, national origin, physical or mental ability, weight, age, gender, or ethnicity. As with serious physical assault and sexual assault, these need legal intervention as well as disciplinary procedures.

To determine what bullying is and what it is not, the following distinctions should be made:

- Cautioning is not bullying, badgering is.
- Coaching is not bullying, humiliating is.
- Disciplining is not bullying, destroying is.
- Competition is not bullying, unhealthy competition is.
- Setting consequences is not bullying, making threats is.
- Holding people accountable is not bullying, seeking revenge is.
- Joking is not bullying, taunting is.
- Flirting is not bullying, stalking is.
- Being tough is not bullying, being mean is.

Cautioning vs. Badgering

If Managers are not able to caution an employee for performance, attitude, behavioral issues without being accused of bullying, they will not be able to effectively do their job.

Good bosses set high expectations and hold employees accountable for their performance, actions and behaviors. It is not bullying when expectations are clear, reasonable, attainable and fair, and employees are provided with the necessary resources, communication and support to achieve their goals. Bosses can be demanding and tough—that should not necessarily label them a bully.

Bosses who set unreasonable and unattainable expectations, and withhold resources, communications and support are bullies. Usually they use harassment and badger people to perform—this is a form of exploitation and is bullying. By demanding results through bullying tactics—they may not be mean, but makes them no less a bully.

Disciplining vs. Destroying

Part of effective performance management is taking disciplinary action up to and including discharge. When this action is taken with the intent to improve performance or correct behaviors or actions it is not bullying. When this action is taken to set up a target it becomes bullying. When targets fall into the bullies trap they give the bully the ammunition they need to take disciplinary action—not to correct, but as you have read in Vera's story, to destroy.

Throughout my career I have had to invite many people out of the organizations I have worked with. Dismissing an employee is one of the most difficult situations a manager has to do. In taking this action it is critical to maintain the person's dignity. It never fails to amaze me how people are destroyed, not so much by this final act but the method by which the action is taken.

Coaching vs. Humiliating

To most readers, the misrepresentation will be quite obvious. A manager who publicly chastises an employee in front of coworkers, emphasizing everything negative about the employee's performance, may defend himself with an assertion that he was coaching the employee. However, the bystanders and the target will probably perceive it for what it is—humiliation—and nothing more. Nothing has been taught, no coaching has taken place. The only result is bad feelings for everyone involved. The difference between coaching and humiliating are obvious. Even professional coaches can fall into this trap, heaping insult onto injury after a defeat. However, when true coaching wins over humiliation the differential between gains and losses is enormous.

A Coaching Moment

Early in my career I had the benefit of having a coach who influenced my management and leadership philosophy for life. Bob McCutheon, was a senior executive at Loblaw Companies Limited (Canada's largest food retailer) appeared in my office early one morning, sat down took out his pipe (they allowed smoking in those days).

As he prepared his pipe (a long drawn out process) he started "Son I have a major problem. You see, there is a young manager; he is cocky, overly aggressive to the point of being abrasive, not sensitive to others, unreasonably demanding, doesn't listen to others, and bullies people to get things done. I'm totally perplexed as what to do." Flattered that Bob, who was considered the senior statesman, would come to me with such a weighty issue, I quickly said, "I would fire the SOB." After taking a long drag from his pipe Bob responding by saying, "Well, son, that's my dilemma. You're the SOB I am talking about."

Thankfully Bob did not follow the advice, but for me it was a lifelong coaching lesson and I went on to become at age twenty-nine the youngest vice president with the organization and enjoyed a twenty-three year career with them.

Competition vs. Unhealthy Competition

Like conflict, competition is a fact of life. We live in a competitive society and it is not altogether a bad thing. Some competition is healthy and some is not.

Healthy competition encourages everyone involved to push themselves harder than they would have without competition, and as a result they achieve more personal or professional growth whether they win or lose. Healthy competition is something that people do together, brings the best out of people, where they learn from each other. Healthy competition expands the boundaries of what you believed was possible for yourself and your group.

Healthy competition celebrates excellence on either side. Healthy competition is motivated out of a love of the game or task, whatever it may be, and doing it well.

Bullying is often at play in unhealthy competition. Unhealthy competition is when a reaction to others' success is negative, rather than inspiring and motivating. Unhealthy competition is where it is hoped that others have limitations because of a fear to lose unless the opponent is somehow held back. Unhealthy competition is where shame is associated with losing rather than the nobility of effort. In unhealthy competition, beating others or being the best is the only goal, and the pressure to win is more important than the fun of playing or learning skills. Unhealthy competition celebrates victory over others, sometimes at any cost. Unhealthy competition is motivated out of a fear of losing, and beating the competition.

How employees are measured, rewarded, recognized, and advanced influences both healthy and unhealthy competition. For example team goals, metrics, and rewards foster healthy competition and heavily weighted individual goals metrics and rewards, the risk of unhealthy competition is there. Also where employees are pitted against each other creates a risk of unhealthy competition.

An example of healthy competition in the workplace would be one in which two teams faced off to solve the same problem. At the end of the competition the teams come together and share their solutions and processes. Competition like this can lead to startling innovation as teams share and learn from each other and lift each other up at the same time.

An example of unhealthy competition in the workplace would be groups or individuals pitted against each other for the approval of a boss. The two sides grow defensive of each other and focus on undermining each as communication breaks down. Feelings of acrimony, hostility, and contempt are planted and the groups employ destructive tactics like sabotage, gossip, and innuendo.

They malign each other on the company intranet and the efforts of the entire department suffer as a result.

∽

An infamous illustration of unhealthy competition is the incident between U.S. Olympic Figure Skating teammates Tonya Harding and Nancy Kerrigan. In January of 1994, in a nefarious display of unhealthy competition, figure skating champion Nancy Kerrigan was literally taken out at the knees by the husband of her rival Tonya Harding, eliminating Kerrigan from the 1994 U.S. Figure Skating Championship. Tonya Harding was subsequently disgraced and after contests with alcohol and impaired driving charges, she took her demons into the ring by launching a female boxing career. Recently Lance Armstrong has brought unhealthy competition to a whole new level.

Holding Accountable vs. Seeking Revenge

People should be held accountable for their words, actions, behaviours and performance. When retaliatory action is taken it becomes revenge.

Consequences vs. Threats

There are good and bad consequences—to outline what could occur in the event or as a result of an action or behaviour is not bullying. When threats are used e.g. "If you don't do this, you will be fired," it is bullying. An example of outlying a consequence is: "Breach of this policy could result in disciplinary action, up to and including discharge."

Joking vs. Taunting

The workplace should be a fun place to be. However, when humor appropriately applied is a great stress reliever and can defuse tense situations. It is okay to poke fun at someone and it is even more effective if you poke fun at yourself. Joking and teasing has to be a give and take—simply put, if you can't take it, don't give it.

One time inappropriate and offensive comments said in jest are not bullying; it becomes bullying when the comments are repeated and used to offend, disparage, insult, demean and ridicule.

In Palm Beach, a former police captain is challenging his demotion to an officer. Two officers claimed that the captain created a hostile work environment by using slurs against women, Jews, racial minorities, gays, and people who are overweight. The offensive behavior is alleged to have occurred over a period of years and six people have lodged discrimination and harassment complaints.

The captain's defense is that he was only joking and he has a "strong sense of humor." A witness in his defense claimed "He's a jovial and joking kind of guy. I've seen people go back and forth, but it is always smiles." It should be noted that this witness was not a target and the people who were did not see the humor.

During my career I have dealt with a number of similar situations and in most cases the person accused usually rationalize the behaviors as "just joking—did not mean to be harmful or malicious," and in all of these cases I found that they were guilty of bullying with the intent to hurt and harm.

Flirting vs. Stalking

Flirting is part of human nature and it would be wrong and impossible to make it illegal in the workplace. Stalking is harassing, with unwanted and obsessive attention. There is a line when flirting starts to become bullying. That line is when it becomes unwanted and if the flirting continues the stalking begins and it is bullying. Most cases can be easily dealt with by the person who is being flirted with simply, by saying something to the effect of,

"I am flattered that you are giving me attention, but it is making me uncomfortable." This unfortunately does not always stop it—usually when the person making the advancements has some power or control over the target.

Toughness vs. Meanness

"Nothing is more despicable than respect based on fear"

—Albert Camus

Tough bosses are often accused of being a bully. Those who are tough and mean usually are. By my definition, being tough is setting high but reasonable expectations and holding people accountable for their performance, behaviours, and actions. I consider myself as being a tough boss, and based on feedback received I have garnered the respect of subordinates. The tough bosses who are mean are not respected—they are feared.

Is There Gender Equality When It Comes To Bullying?

I am often asked, do men bully more than women or do men bully women more than other men? Or do women bully other women more than they bully men?

Based on research conducted by Dr. Gary Namie of the Workplace Bullying Institute, women are equally responsible for bullying behaviors, men bully women more than they bully men, and women similarly bully other women more than they target men. Further, the Institute has found that 80% of bullying by female bosses is directed at other women.

During my career I have mentored a number of women as they advanced to managers and executives. As most organizations are still dominated by males, it is a challenge for women to break through the glass ceiling, and most of the women I have worked with have had to fight their way to the top echelons of management.

Women are conditioned to be tough in order to progress (even survive) in male dominated organizations. Also in these environments women have to meet higher standards on proving their toughness than their male peers. Again, as indicated earlier, being tough should not be considered to be a negative attribute. It is, however, when it is being tough and mean.

Clearly a double standard exists; when a woman asserts herself, even if she is not a bully, she is very likely going to be called a bitch or be told that she is being emotional. When a man is tough, but not a bully, he usually garners respect and when he bullies, it is usually rationalized as "doing what he has to do to get things done."

When women react to comments, situations, or actions they find offensive people may make a comment like, "If you can't take the heat, get out of the kitchen."

Bottom line, women have had to develop a thicker skin than men to advance, and in so doing, often fall into *The Bully's Trap*—in essence becoming a bullied bully.

Again, based on my experience, there is a double standard applied as both male targets of the bullying and organizations are less tolerant when women bully men than a male bully.

A dynamic commonly at play in women bullying women is the motive of eliminating a real or perceived threat. Common ways this is manifested is discrediting through gossip and innuendo or exclusion.

Studies have shown that when women who progress in an organization have less talent than some of their subordinates, it is usually because they are viewed as tougher or they have garnered favors or the subtle approval to bully from their bosses or they have learned to manipulate the social fabric of the office to their own favour. These women often know they have less talent than the women they are excluding and so view their bullying as the means to keep their positions, both professional and social. Organizations who have implemented affirmative action programs or quotas have often promoted women with less talent than some of their subordinates.

Studies have also shown that women will bully other women who are a direct threat to their bosses or men they admire in the organization.

One comment that someone made resonated greatly with women I have spoken to on the topic: "If there are two women in a board meeting and ten men, the two women will view each other as the greatest threat, than any of the men."

Sexual Bullying

"Can you espouse the values of fairness and respect, and at the same time discriminate and injure? Sexist and sexually harassing behaviours are dissatisfying and therefore undesirable actions that hurt people and are unworthy of people of intelligence and integrity."

—Peter Milner
Sexual Respect Curriculum

As there is an abundance of published material on sexual harassment and how it is defined and the impacts, there is no need for me to expand on what already exists. I will rather focus on the dynamics of sexual bullying in the workplace.

Where there is sexual harassment in the workplace, like other forms of bullying, it is usually boss to subordinate and where the person making the advancements has some power or control over the target.

In the many cases of sexual bullying I have dealt with over my career, most were women who were bullied by a boss who believed he was entitled by virtue of the position he held and often emboldened, knowing the target would be afraid to report. In most cases, threats or promises were made, usually sexual favours were sought in exchange for extra pay and/or promotions.

While the majority of cases are male bosses bullying female subordinates, male and female bosses also target male subordinates for sexual favours.

The US Equal Employment Opportunity Commission (EEOC) has reported that while there has been a gradual decline of grievances filed, there is an increase of complaints filed by men.

A 2008 telephone poll by Louis Harris and Associates on 782 US workers revealed:

- 31% of the female workers reported they had been harassed at work
- 7% of the male workers reported they had been harassed at work
- 62% of targets took no action
- 100% of the women reported the harasser was a man
- 59% of men reported the harasser was a woman
- 41% of men reported the harasser was another man

Of the women who had been harassed:

- 43% were harassed by a supervisor
- 27% were harassed by an employee senior to them
- 19% were harassed by a co worker at their level
- 8% were harassed by a junior employee

The following illustrates the impacts and attitudes on sexual bullying in the workplace.

Australian Publicist, Kristy Fraser-Kirk accused her boss, Mark McInness of making unwanted sexual advances. In their August 2, 2010 article, Robert Fenner and Joe Schneider reported that after the lawsuit was filed, her "whole life has been turned upside down." In her complaint she said McInness put his hand under her clothes at a May luncheon and, that after a June party, he urged her to go to his home, with the clear implication that such a visit would be for the purpose of sexual intercourse.

Although the company had a strong harassment policy in place, obviously the procedures were not followed. Fraser-Kirk's immediate supervisor and the general manager of public relations told her simply to tell the CEO to back off if it happened again. The CEO resigned in June, stating, "As a chief executive officer and as a person I have a responsibility to many, and today I formally acknowledge that I have committed serious errors of judgment and have inexcusably let down the female staff member." He never acknowledged what he had actually done. And one must ask, "Since when is sexual bullying merely a case of 'letting down a female staff member?'" He left David Jones with more than $8.6 million in cash and shares. He was then hired as the CEO of Solomon Lew's Premier Investments retail business with an annual salary of $2 million plus bonuses that could amount to $3.2 million.

In a final settlement of the lawsuit. Fraser-Kirk received a settlement of $850,000 with the company paying $470,000 and McInnes paying the rest. This is the largest sexual harassment settlement in Australian corporate to date.

Shortly after the Australian department store chain, David Jones, its board and the former CEO, Mark McInness were hit with this sexual harassment suit, a survey of 505 women by the cosmetic company, Heat Group, found that 44 percent of Australian women have been sexually harassed at work, and 62 percent didn't think companies were doing enough to support those who have been harassed. More than three quarters of the woman believed the management were aware of the harassment but failed to do anything.

༄

An example of how difficult it is for targets to report is that of Virginia Messick, one of sixty-two trainees who were victims of assault or other improper conduct by thirty-two instructors in 2011 at Lackland Air Force Base in San Antonio, Texas.

Virginia did not initially report being raped because the protocol for reporting required that she report it to the person who attacked her.

Case Study—The Ethic of Reciprocity—Linda's Story

Linda is a single mother who has worked as an Administrative Assistant for a Not For Profit Agency for twelve years. Linda's boss, Eric is the Executive Director who joined the agency five years ago at age sixty-five after retiring as a senior executive with a major Pharmaceutical firm.

Eric and Linda enjoyed an excellent working relationship and Eric was always sensitive and responsive to the pressures that Linda faced as a single mom and always accommodated her when she needed to come in late or leave early to attend to her daughter.

Although Linda earned a decent wage, money was tight, she had a mortgage on a condo she bought a few years ago, her car was nine years old and repair costs were starting to cost more than it was worth. Linda's ex is a dead beat, and has not provided any financial support since they separated.

In late 2007 Linda was diagnosed with cancer. The prognoses was good, however, she required an operation and the drug regimentation required her to be absent from work at least a week a month for eight to twelve months.

Linda's benefits with the agency did not include short term disability and the drug therapy prescribed was not of the formulary of the medical plan she purchased. Linda felt that there were few options. None of her family members had the capacity to support her through this, nor could her friends. Perhaps if she went to them they could all chip in and collect enough to cover her, but she was not optimistic.

Desperate, Linda went to Eric and laid out the situation. Eric responded immediately by telling her not to worry, he would figure something out. "Your main focus has to be on getting better," he assured her.

The next day Eric told her that she could take off as much time as she needed, with pay, and the agency would pay for her drug therapy and if she required home care or someone to take care of her daughter while she was being treated, the agency would pay for this as well. Linda was so relieved that she jumped up and gave Eric a big hug.

In early 2008 the tumor was successfully removed and she started the therapy. The side effects were relatively moderate, yet it did require that she be off work for six or seven days after each treatment.

During this period, Eric was wonderful, he not only delivered on his promises, he supported Linda emotionally as well, always asking how she was feeling, inquiring how her daughter was coping and telling her if there was anything else she needed, all she had to do was ask.

In March of 2008 Eric invited Linda out for dinner to discuss the agenda for the next board meeting. That Thursday they had dinner at the Ruth Chris Steakhouse which was located near their office. After going over the agenda for the meeting they exchanged stories about their background, families and friends. Eric confided that his marriage of forty seven years was not a happy one and he was very lonely for companionship. When they went to their cars, Eric asked Linda if they could meet for dinner on a regular basis. While this raised a bit of a red flag with Linda, she agreed thinking, "it's the least I can do after everything he has done for me."

For the next few weeks Eric and Linda had dinner except for the weeks that she was in treatment. Even though Eric was old enough to be her father, Linda quite enjoyed his company, he was caring, witty and had the energy of a man twenty years his junior.

In May, Eric indicated that he would be attending a conference in Atlanta and invited Linda along, "It will be good for your professional development. Linda thought it was unusual for Eric to make the hotel arrangements but once they arrived, she found out why. Checking in Linda was aghast that Eric only made arrangements for one room they had to share. Once they got into the room Linda objected. Eric became irritated and said "you don't have a choice here, have you never heard of the ethic of reciprocity?" Linda was upset and confused "What do you mean?" she asked. "Let's face it, I am helping you and now you are going to help me" Eric answered. He continued by saying "You have a choice here, you can leave, but if you do, it's over, I will fire you."

It started that day, Linda had to submit to Eric's demands to save her job and continue to receive financial support for her condition. If she did not have her daughter to think about she would have walked out. Linda also realised that given the overall economic situation and her medical condition she would not be able to find another job.

For a man in his early seventies Eric had an insatiable appetite for sex and he became increasingly demanding, insisting that they get together at a sleazy motel at least twice a week. Linda's only reprieve was when she was in therapy. Even then he tried to convince her to meet. Also, Eric's tastes went from vanilla to kink.

This went on until November of 2009. Linda was at the breaking point. A number of times she almost called the Chair of the Board of the agency but decided against it as Eric and the Chair were very close and Eric indicated that if she told anyone he would claim that she initiated "the affair."

In the last week of November Eric drove Linda to a new location. They went into a building that looked like a warehouse. Once they got inside Linda discovered that it was a sex club, in the center of the room was a huge mattress with a number of people engaged in all kinds of revolting activities. "Here is the deal," Eric said, "We are going to check our clothing in the locker room, then I want you to join in the group, while I watch."

Linda had had enough, and she ran to the entrance and got out. Fortunately she was able to grab a cab and asked the driver to take her home. Once she got home Linda called the police who came over immediately.

Eric was charged with sexual assault and his case is still pending. The Board of Directors asked for and received his resignation.

Linda continues to work for the agency. Eric's replacement is a former Board member and she and Linda have a good working relationship. Being a cancer survivor, the new Executive Director was able to relate to what Linda was going through medically, however she like others could not imagine the horror Linda suffered by following Eric's distorted view of the "ethic of reciprocity."

Sexual Orientation and Bullying in the Workplace

"Keeping executives from coming out are homophobic corporate cultures and boards"

—John Brown
former CEO, BP PLC

Over the last decade, much progress has been made in shifting attitudes towards sexual orientation.

Notwithstanding the progress made, even in enlightened organizations, homosexual and transgender workers are fearful of either coming out or being outed.

This is not surprising as companies in twenty nine of the US states can still fire a worker for being gay. Also according to the Human Rights Campaign, there is not a single openly gay CEO in the Fortune 1000 companies.

In 2007 BP PLC Chief John Brown resigned amid revelations he had lied in court on how he met his boyfriend. In a Wall Street Journal article on July 25, 2011, by Leslie Kwoh called "A Silence That Hangs Over CEO's", Brown stated, "Keeping executives from coming out are homophobic corporate cultures and Boards" and "companies are very conservative and the bigger the business is, the more conservative it is."

Similarly, in professional sports, very few athletes have had the courage to come out. Mark Tewksbury the Canadian Olympic Gold Medallist in swimming stated at the 2009 Vancouver Q Hall of Fame launch, "It's a difficult place to be if you are straight." "Sport is still a top down from policy makers," he told Xtra, Canada's GLBT magazine, adding, "it's very dogmatic and rule bound. People don't want to change rule structures. It's by nature, highly conservative. It's pretty much the last machinations of the old boys club."

Until Jason Collins, a veteran of 12 NBA seasons, announced in April of 2013 that he was gay there were no openly gay athletes in the NFL, NBL, and MLB. In soccer Robbie Rodgers, the former member of the US National Team, revealed on his blog in February that he was gay. Had he announced earlier, he would have been the first openly gay male athlete to play in a major American team sport.

Very few in broadcasting have come out, a rare exception being CNN's Anderson Cooper who did so in July 2012.

In entertainment, a 2012 survey by the actors union Equity revealed that only 57% of gay actors felt they could be open about their sexually with their agent and one third had experienced homophobia in the workplace, saying it had come from other performers.

In the United States, the Southern Poverty Law Center examined the total number of hate crimes (criminal bullying) against persons compiled by the FBI for the years 1995–2008. They then compared the rate of targeting of homosexuals to that of five other groups and found that homosexuals are 2.4 times more likely to suffer a violent hate crime attack than Jews; 2.6 times more than blacks, 4.4 times than Muslims, 13.8 times more likely than Latinos; and 41.5 times more than whites.

For years, race discrimination claims have led all other types of claims filed, however much what I found in research on hate crimes in the workplace was that sexual orientation discrimination was ahead of all of them.

The Williams Institute on Sexual Orientation Law and Public Policy pulled together a number of surveys on discrimination and harassment of gay and transgender workers. The results:

a. "15 to 43 percent of gay and transgender workers have experienced some form of discrimination on the job.

b. 8 to 17 percent of gay and transgender workers report being passed over for a job or fired because of their sexual orientation or gender identity.

c. 10 to 28 percent received a negative performance evaluation or were passed over for a promotion because they were gay or transgender.

d. 7 to 41 percent of gay and transgender workers were verbally or physically abused or had their workplace vandalized.

e. 12 to 30 percent of straight workers witnessed discrimination in the workplace based on sexual orientation."

The 2011 comprehensive study on transgender discrimination by the National Center for Transgender Equality and the National Gay and Lesbian Task Force found:

- "90 percent of transgender individuals have encountered some form of harassment or mistreatment on the job

- 47 percent were passed over for a job and/or denied a promotion

- 26 percent had lost a job because they were transgender."

Case Study—No Way Out—Mark's Story

Mark worked for a midsized medical equipment company for twenty-two years, he started as an inventory control clerk working his way up and was recently promoted to head of purchasing. He joined the company after graduating from the local community college. The company is located in a mid western city where Mark grew up. Mark and Lori married the year after he graduated college. Their two sons are now in their late teens.

In 2009 Mark was found dead in his car, which was parked in his garage, from carbon monoxide poisoning. Mark committed suicide.

While Mark's suicide came as a total shock to Lori and their sons, they knew there was something wrong for a long time, but did not know what. For two or so years prior Mark was not himself, he was withdrawn, irritable, depressed, lethargic, suffered stomach disorders headaches restless at night, unable to sleep, kept to himself and when asked what was going on would always answer, "Nothing really, just a bit of pressure at work," and told them that there was nothing to worry about.

Shortly after the funeral, John, a close friend of Mark's, asked to meet with Lori, indicating that he had some information that she should be aware of and would answer why Mark had taken his life.

When they met, John was very distraught and said "If I had done something earlier, Mark would be alive today." John indicated to Lori that Mark asked him to tell Lori the whole story after "he left."

John told Lori that Mark approached him a month before he died to ask John for help, that he had no one else to turn to. Mark indicated to John that he had done something terrible and needed to make it right and he had to get out of the situation he had found himself in. Based on what Mark told him, John assumed that "getting out" meant that Mark was going to run away.

John started from the beginning.

Mark's manager Ed was also a long service employee with the Company. Mark and Ed had a reasonable working relationship but not close socially outside of work. Ed was pretty rough around the edges and could be very crude when things upset him. Mark learned to live with it and rationalized Ed's behavior like everybody else did in the company by saying or thinking "Oh, that's just Ed."

In early 2006 Ed called Mark into his office and said "I hear you are a f—ing faggot, somebody told me that you are a regular at some queer joint called the Red Rooster." (The Red Rooster is a gay establishment in a neighbouring city.) Mark was flabbergasted and said "I don't know what you are talking about, and even if I was, it is none of your business." Ed then pulled out three photos and said "You're not only a f—ing faggot but you're a f—ing liar. You work for me and it is my f—ing business."

Mark was devastated. Not only did he risk losing his family should his sexuality become known, he feared for his own physical safety. Homosexuals in the Midwest have lost their lives. Only a decade earlier, Matthew Shepard, a young man from Wyoming was beaten and left for dead hanging on a barbed wire fence, after frequenting a gay bar.

This information from Ed floored Mark. He asked "Who else knows?" Ed smiled and said "I always knew you were a pansy, so I decided to have you followed, the only other person is a private investigator who is paid to keep his mouth shut." Ed then proceeded to tell Mark that he had a little scheme in mind and if Mark wanted "Our little secret" kept that way, he would have to play along. Ed then ended the meeting by saying "I will lay it out to you tomorrow." thus began Mark's nightmare.

During his high school years Mark knew he was attracted to men. Mark resisted the temptations and felt that it was a passing phase. In grade twelve he started dating Lori who was a year behind him. The city they lived in was small, fairly close knit and there were no opportunities for Mark to explore what he became to realise was not a passing phase. Mark was as closeted as one could be.

Ten or so years after Mark and Lori married, Mark attended a conference in Atlanta. It was there he met John who coincidentally was from the same city and alumni of the college Mark had attended. Mark and John recognized each other and decided to have dinner. Over dinner they realized a mutual attraction and spent the remainder of the conference together. John was also married at the time and while not as closeted as Mark, he kept his sexuality a secret. Mark and John carried on an affair for less than two years and decided they should end it but remain close friends, which they were. John was the only person Mark could be "out" with and John introduced him to "the scene" in the neighbouring city.

After the confrontation with Ed, Mark was petrified. He had been so careful to protect his secret, now his worst fears were becoming reality. Mark was convinced that if he were exposed he would lose everything, Lori would leave him, his sons would disown him, it could kill his ailing parents, he would be shunned by the community and Ed would find a way to force him out of the company. All night he wondered what Ed had in mind to keep "our little secret" kept that way.

Early the next morning Ed was already in Mark's office waiting for Mark. "Let's go for a ride," Ed suggested. In Ed's car, Ed laid out the "scheme."

"I will keep our little secret if you arrange for ten of our vendors to give us kickbacks, if you don't I will go to Jim (the CFO who was Ed's boss) and tell him that you approached me with the idea to keep me quiet, because you found out I knew you were a faggot." Mark had to have Ed stop the car, he quickly opened the door and threw up what little he had eaten for dinner the night before. What Ed was demanding went totally against Mark's value system. He prided himself on the relationships he had developed with the vendor community and now he was being blackmailed to betray the company he loved, the vendor community and himself.

"I can't do it," Mark declared.

"You don't have much of a choice pansy boy, if you don't, you are going to be fired, and everyone will find out that you are a faggot who tried to keep it a secret by bribing me to do something illegal. Nobody will hire you again I'll see to it, you will be on the street." "Give me a couple of days to think about it" Mark asked. "Take your time, faggot," Ed responded.

Mark did not know what to do. He considered discussing it with Lori but he could not take the risk. The only person he could talk to about it was John, but what could John do other than lend a sympathetic ear. Mark seriously considered suicide at the time but decided that was a coward's way out.

Two days later Ed was waiting for Mark in his office. "Let's go for another ride" Ed suggested. This time they drove the local gym that they both belonged to. They met in the dry sauna where they could be alone.

"Now here is how it works, I will give you the names of ten vendors who I know will co-operate. All you have to do is give them an amount to deposit each month in an offshore account and each month you will transfer the entire balance to another offshore account. I will give you instructions on how and where to open the account and the instructions on how to automatically have the balance in your account transferred to my account."

It started that week. Mark met with each vendor in a safe environment and they all agreed to the terms. Mark knew that this type of thing went on but had no idea, based on the reaction of the vendors, how it was almost expected. It was obvious to Mark that he was not the first person Ed recruited to engage in this type of activity. Ed always wondered how Ed could afford living in a multimillion dollar house, a stay at home wife, the expensive cars and exotic trips. Now he knew. He also wondered if the higher ups in the company questioned Ed's extravagant lifestyle.

The other thing that perplexed Mark was the lack of checks and balances in place to avoid this type of activity. All an auditor would have to do is a net/net price comparison and it would show that they were overpaying for many items.

For close to the next three years, Marks life was a living hell. Not only was he engaged in this illegal activity, which, if he was caught, would land him in jail for a long time, but at every opportunity, when no one was within ear shot, Ed would call him a "f—ing faggot" or "pansy boy." Ed would also question Mark about his relationship with Lori and offer to "service her" as "obviously she is not getting it from you."

During this period Ed became greedier and greedier. Periodically Ed would arrange for them to meet in the dry sauna at the gym, again to make sure no one could listen and make sure Mark was not wired. Even though Ed was a boorish goon, he was not stupid. At these meetings Ed would add to the vendor list and increase the amounts the others were paying. The total amount collected over this period exceeded seven million dollars.

From the beginning Mark kept a diary of every discussion he had with Ed and the vendors. He also had a record of each and every transaction. At some point he was going to expose Ed, the only problem is he did not know how.

Finally he figured it out. He would engage his friend, John. They met at John's house and Mark laid out the full story, giving John a copy of his diary and a record of all of the transactions. Mark indicated to John that "there was only one way to end this, I have to leave." John tried to convince Mark that he should go to the CEO of the company with this, to which Mark replied, "I just can't face him; this is my only way out."

Mark asked John to meet with Lori, "after I leave," and tell her the whole story. Mark indicated he wanted it to be Lori's decision on whether to go to the CEO of the company with the diary and the records.

A month later, Mark got out.

Lori quietly listened to the whole story. "Now it all makes sense," she commented. "I knew from the beginning that Mark was bisexual," she told John. "I also knew the two of you had a thing going, but I still loved him, we were best friends, had a wonderful relationship, and he was a great Dad." Lori also indicated that being bi or gay was not a choice, the choice was whether to be out or not and Mark made his choice which Lori respected because she knew that Mark believed if he came out it would hurt her and their sons.

Lori decided, after consulting with her sons, who wholeheartedly concurred that she and John needed to go to the CEO of the company and relay the full story.

The CEO readily agreed to meet with them. At the meeting he listened to the story, read the diary and reviewed the records of the transactions. After he was finished, he wept and said, "I don't know how Mark was able to bear this burden for as long as he did. Lori, I am so ashamed of what happened here and that Mark did not feel comfortable enough in coming to me with this."

"I would like to have a week to determine what to do," the CEO said, adding that he would like to meet with Lori and John again after the week. He also gave them an assurance that Mark's name and reputation would be protected in whatever action they decided to take.

That week the CEO met with the Chair of the Board of Directors and the Chair of Audit, gave them the full story and offered his resignation which they indicated would not be necessary and they indicated that they too had to accept some responsibility for not having the checks and balances in place.

As promised the CEO met with Lori and John the following week to outline what the Board had decided.

A forensic audit was conducted that found that the kickbacks dated back to two years after Ed started with the Company.

Ed was charged, convicted, sent to prison, and ordered to make full restitution.

All of the vendors involved avoided criminal charges by making full restitution and paying the company penalties for their actions.

The CFO's resignation was accepted. The CEO and the Board viewed him as being negligent.

Checks and balances were put in place and periodic audits are conducted to avoid prevent this type of thing from happening in the future.

Lori will continue to receive Mark's compensation until he would have reached retirement age after which she will receive his full pension benefits.

Mark and Lori's sons will receive full scholarships to a university of their choice from the company.

Mark's reputation was protected.

Hazing

> Hazing is a complex social problem that is shaped by power dynamics operating in a group and/or organization and within a particular cultural context.
>
> —StopHazing.org, Educating to Eliminate

In a March 9, 2010 report on hazing in the Mississauga, Ontario Transportation and Works Department, the following were some of the incidents detailed:

a. "Two male employees were bound face-to-face with duct tape on top of a large table in the sign workshop. Other employees threw water balloons at them.

b. An employee was wrapped up with duct tape, thrown in the back of a truck, and driven through a car wash.

c. On his birthday, an employee was told to lean over a table; other workers were instructed in turn to hit him, allegedly to "hit hard and kick or punch in the face, ribs or groin area. If the blows were not hard enough, the workers were told to hit harder."

The city was notified about the hazings in November of 2009 and ordered an investigation resulting in "changes to workplace harassment policies" but no one was suspended then. Even after a "full investigation" the city manager stated that, "the behavior was in the nature of horseplay…locker room behavior." After the investigation by the city's HR department, the Ontario Ministry of Labor reviewed the case, but still no disciplinary action was taken against the perpetrators. The Peel Regional Police investigated and reported they could not file charges as "eyewitnesses said that the employees involved in the hazing incidents consented to the activity."

However, once cell phone video footage of one of the hazing incidents was made public, a further investigation resulted in two supervisors being suspended without pay and required to submit written apologies to residents of Mississauga, the staff, and the city council. The same city manager who called the incidents "horseplay" and "locker room behavior" was now saying that she was "disgusted and appalled" by its contents and "in no way do we condone this type of behavior." Mayor Hazel McCallion stated that, "As you can appreciate, it's completely unacceptable. It is contrary to the code of conduct of the employees of the city of Mississauga and the necessary disciplinary action has been taken. The employees have been warned and if any action near this were to happen again, they would be terminated by the city, such actions should not happen on city property and on taxpayers' money."

The employee who provided the cell phone video footage and filed the complaint with the Ministry of Labor against the Mississauga Transportation and Works Department was quoted in the Toronto Star, June 3, 2010: "I can assure you it's more than horseplay. It's oppression. We live in fear. I've complained repeatedly to no avail. People are afraid of coming forward to report the abuse and it is fear that compelled people to take part in hazing....It's so serious, we fear for more than just our jobs. (We) fear for our safety, safety of the people I love."

He and other workers confirmed that some employees had been beaten and abused by other workers for about five years. Most said they went along with the hazing for fear of reprisal or being fired. An employee asking the question "Why didn't these [targets] fight back?" answered his own question with "I guess they had no choice. They were overpowered." Yet, some other employees said it was just "practical jokes," and was "appreciated, good-natured, and voluntary." In a blog attached to the Toronto Star story, a blogger commented, "...these guys are only trying to make their work environment a little more fun and now [the whistleblower] has taken all of the fun out of the job."

As is typical in so many workplace hazing incidents, in the Mississauga case, the person who reported the hazing received some support and affirmation of the abusive antics from some coworkers who had been targeted themselves, while others wrote it off as practical jokes, a supervisor participated in the hazing and concluded no harm was done. The lack of support by the supervisor, the dismissal of the complaint by the city manager, and the coworker backlash against the whistleblower compounded the humiliation and pain of the original incident.

Just as taunting is not teasing and sexual bullying is not flirting, hazing is more than horseplay. Hazing is abusive and degrading; it creates a climate of fear and breeds mistrust and apathy. Often written off as "harmless office antics," it has all of the markers of bullying:

1. "power (the target of the hazing being outnumbered or lower on the social and/or employment ladder than those doing the hazing);

2. wanting to harm (being forced to eat food with hands behind their backs as servers at a Hooters restaurant were made to do while other workers and the manager looked on laughing; caging a worker and taunting him with racial slurs; forcing an employee to wear embarrassing or humiliating attire; being beaten or forced to beat a coworker are all done to get pleasure from someone else's pain or humiliation);

3. threaten (whether stated or implied, 'do it or else,' is the message received by the target of the hazing)"

In a study conducted in April 2000 Alfred University Study, hazing was defined as "any activity expected of someone joining a group that humiliates, degrades, abuses or endangers, regardless of the person's willingness to participate. " This can include activities that on the surface appear benign but are done where "an atmosphere of humiliation, degradation, abuse, or danger exists." Speaking about the "risk of initiations that include being humiliated or forced to engage in illegal or dangerous activities." One of the researchers, Professor of Anthropology, Robert Meyers commented: "Our culture views hazing as 'fun and exciting.' America's obsession with 'fun' apparently gives us license to justify almost any type of behavior, no matter how abusive." The principal investigator, Nadine Hoover, noted: "We anticipated that we would find some level of hazing. What we found distressing was the prevalence."

The pervasiveness of hazing in middle school, high school, university and the workplace points to a cultural acceptance of hazing even as we decry bullying in our schools and in our workplaces. In a blog attached to the Toronto Star story, a blogger commented, "…these guys are only trying to make their work environment a little more fun and now [the whistleblower] has taken all of the fun out of the job." We have to wonder why it is considered "fun and exciting" to demean another human being at work in order to make the work environment a "little more fun." We speak out of both sides of our mouth when we tell employees to treat one another with dignity and regard, then encourage or condone hazing, calling it "character building," or "practical jokes," or "horseplay."

No criminal charges could be laid in the Mississauga incident because eyewitnesses said that those who were hazed "consented." However, since consent of the target can no longer be used as a defense in civil or criminal suits in jurisdictions that have anti-hazing (or anti-bullying) laws, as the law recognizes that it may not be actual consent when considering the pressure employees face when the offender is a supervisor or a supervisor and his or her/ henchmen, or a group of coworkers who could easily make the workplace even more hostile for the one who does not "consent" to the hazing. Fear of being ostracized, further hazed, or fired does not make it easy for someone to object. The question should not be "Did he consent?" Rather, "Is the activity that is required demeaning, humiliating, abusive, and/ or degrading?" A second question that can affirm that the activity is hazing— "Who is having the fun and at who's expense?" If the perpetrators are laughing at the target's humiliation, pain, or degradation it is a sure sign that the activity is not merely horseplay or a practical joke; it is hazing.

Why Bullies Bully

Bullies bully because they can. As you have seen in Part One, most organizations allow, condone, encourage, and even expect their managers to bully.

Our research and that of others show that the main reason people are targeted is to force them out.

The usual motivations and intentions are:

- To reduce labor costs
- Retaliation to punish the target
- Bigotry
- Exploitation—to get people to work harder and faster (it is the only way weak managers know how to manage)
- To exercise (abuse) their power
- To eliminate a threat

Reduce Labor Costs

Almost every day we hear in the media about questionable business practices. One area that needs to be exposed is organizations using bullying tactics to reduce employment costs. Older workers and long term employees are particularly vulnerable. The formula is very simple; force senior employees out and replace them with younger ones, at a lower pay rate thereby reducing the overall average salary. If people quit, severance is avoided. By doing this there is an added benefit for those companies who have a defined benefit plan, their pension costs and unfunded liability is greatly reduced. While I do not want to debate the false economics of this, we only want to expose it for what it is, ethically and morally dishonest and wrong.

Precedence on this will be based on the outcome of two class action suits that Federal Express is facing. The two suits claim that Fed Ex has actual policies and practices in place that are designed to push employees out before they reach age fifty-five. The plaintiffs in the case allege that Fed Ex discriminates against couriers over forty years old, especially if they have over ten years' seniority, by taking away their routes and setting unrealistic performance targets, and that the company gave supervisors lists of older workers to target for increased supervision, discipline, and harassment.

The Workplace Bullying Institute in their 2007 study found that for 77 percent of the bullying targets, the only way they could stop the bullying was to leave their employment.

Retaliation

Bullies are vindictive, not only toward their targets who try to stand up to them, but also towards those who call them on it.

While many employers claim to have an open door policy and tools in place such as a whistleblower hot line, not all welcome contrary viewpoints and reports of irregularities or wrongdoing. Some shoot the messenger and retaliate against employees who don't follow the party line, who fight an injustice, or who report irregularities or wrong doing.

The Workplace Bullying Institute in their "How Employers and Coworkers Respond to Workplace Bullying—Labor Day 2008" report, found that of those that report bullying, employers predominately did nothing (53 percent) and actually retaliated against the person (71 percent) who dared report it. Filing complaints led to retaliation by the employer of bullied targets leading to lost jobs (24 percent). In 46 percent of bullying cases, coworkers abandoned their bullied colleagues, to the extent that 15 percent aggressed against the target along with the bully.

My experience with companies who have whistleblower hot lines is that executives and boards are proud of how few calls are made to the hotline without even considering that employees and vendors may not trust the system.

In 2009, retaliation moved up to tie with race discrimination as the most common type of charge filed with the U.S. Equal Employment Opportunity Commission (EEOC).

Even in the United States, which lags behind all westernized jurisdictions on anti-bullying legislation, the Supreme Court has issued a declaration that changes the grounds on which retaliation claims are actionable. With the Burlington Northern vs. White decision of the U.S. Supreme Court (2006) the increased action is likely to keep growing. By making this decision the court has effectively broadened the standard to be allowed in unlawful retaliation claims made against employers so that courts will now apply a different standard for analyzing adverse employment action in retaliation cases than discrimination cases.

The demise of organizations and the global meltdown could have been avoided had people in the know reported the wrong doing—they did not, largely for fear of being retaliated against. In most cases the whistleblowers are viewed as traders and subject to bullying as punishment for their crime.

According to over ten thousand cases from the UK and National Work Advice Line in cases reported through its website, the fifth reason for being bullied is "blowing the whistle on malpractice fraud, illegal legalities, breaches of rules, regulations and procedures, or raising health and safety issues."

In the appendix I have included an article written by Richard Alderson one of my Associates at Iceburg Navigation, called "Whistleblowers Protection: Creeping Towards a Solution", which provides a compressive review of the topic and more importantly what organizations must do to make it safe for people to come forward and report wrong doing.

Bigotry

Despite the huge amounts of money organizations have spent on diversity and sensitivity training, people are still targeted merely because they are different in some way. Bullies need targets on whom they can heap their aggression on, and the differences identified as the justifications for the attacks are spurious at best, contemptuous at worse.

Race discrimination ties retaliation as the most common type of charge filed with the U.S. Equal Opportunity Commission.

International Communications Research conducted a phone survey of 623 randomly selected employed Americans in February of 2006 indicated:

- 30 percent overheard racial slurs
- 20 percent reported ridicule of perceived or sexual orientation
- 20 percent experienced age bias
- 35 percent of men and 28 percent of women overheard abuses from the highest level.

Exploitation and Weak Management

"All cruelty springs from weakness"

—Seneca

Where there is ambiguity and subjectivity in an organizations performance management process, there are opportunities for the bully to misuse the management process to wreck havoc with the targeted employee's work performance.

A host of European studies found that many of the environmental characteristics that contribute to bullying are actually describing the functional features of a work unit and most of them are also factors related to leadership style and supervisory practices. Heinz Leymann commented in his article, "The Content and Development of Mobbing at Work," that of the 800 case studies where mobbing (UK term for bullying) occurred frequently, an almost stereotypical pattern of poorly organized working methods and weak management were found.

Research suggests that overloaded and bullied employees tend to work for organizations that are declining or shrinking, where the management style is bureaucratic and reactive.

Like the bullied character Vera in Vera's Story, being bullied affects their performance. This is understandable given the trauma experienced daily by the person who is targeted. The real tragedy here is that deterioration of performance and being absent because of the stress of bullying or a shift in attitude gives the bully ammunition to discipline up to and including discharging the bullied employee, with the sanction and encouragement of the organization. This is a huge catch twenty-two for bullied employees and a huge enabler for the bully—"*The Bully's Trap.*"

Kaj Bjorkqvist, Karin Osterman, and Monika Hjelt-Back in 'Aggression Among University Employees' wrote: "Like domestic violence, it can be difficult for people to talk about workplace bullying." This has made it difficult to capture the true dimensions of the problem, and helps explain why it is not always recognized. Like any abusive relationship, people tend to deny or minimize abuse as a way to survive it. The workplace provides a further wrinkle in that bullying behavior can be easily concealed by or disguised as "strong management." Likewise, it is difficult for targets to report, as targets risk retribution and job loss. It can also have a stigmatizing effect, since to admit to being harassed at work is something others might see as a weakness or an inability to cope.

Abuse of Power

"Power over a man's subsistence amounts to power over his will."

—Alexander Hamilton

People who have power and have to rely on their position to get others to do things, or not do things are bullies and this is abuse of power, particularly if people are forced into doing things that unethical or in conflict with their values and beliefs.

In the media, reports of corruption by executives and politicians have become commonplace. What is common in most of the stories we hear about is how long the corruption has gone on without people in the know coming forward. There is few or no question that these people were bullied into silence.

In organizations where there are no checks and balances, bullies can and do target employees purely to assert their power. Again, 70 percent of bullying is boss to subordinate—and the boss has the power of position and is in a position to use power to instill fear.

Although it is common for coworkers to bully their colleagues, it is more often top down. When it starts at the top it does impact the entire organizational culture.

Eliminating a Threat

Many bullies are insecure despite their confident façade. Bullies have no qualms about getting rid of a subordinate or coworker who might make them look bad, usurp his power, is smarter—or more attractive, younger, older, or those who receive more attention from superiors—in essence anyone who is a threat to their power and status.

During my career, I have been involved in a number of reorganizations. As reorganizations usually involve massive change—it also usually triggers reactions from those who fear losing power and control.

Case Study—They Wanted To Push Me Out—William's Story

In 2007 William quit his job as a driver for a major transportation and logistics company after twelve years of employment. At the time William was forty three years old. William thought that he would have no problem finding another job, however, with the economic downturn and the unemployment rate in southern California reaching double digit, this was not the case. At the time of writing this book, William was still out of work. Recently he and his family moved in with his in-laws as the house that they had lived in for eight years went into foreclosure. There is a bit of income coming in from William's wife who works part time for a National Drug Chain. There is some hope that William may be able to get his job back and be paid for the period he has been off as his union has filed a grievance on his behalf and for a number of others who either quit or were fired.

Until 2006 William thought that he would be a lifer with the Company. The Company provided good wages and benefits and had a defined pension plan. Working conditions were excellent and the vehicles were always clean and in good working order. The company prided itself on their employee relations and wanted to be known as "an employer of choice," they had a huge Human Resources Department and all of the "state of the art" employment policies, procedures and practices. The majority of employees were represented by a union.

In 2006 the company negotiated a new collective agreement with the union. The main changes were; a two tier wage and benefit structure, and a change in the pension plan from a defined benefit to a defined contribution. Existing employees maintained their wage grid and benefit coverage and had the option of switching their pension to the defined contribution plan. New hires after the agreement was ratified would go on the new grid and the much reduced benefit plan and the defined contribution pension plan.

Almost immediately after the new collective agreement went into effect there was a major restructuring at the supervisory level and Geoff, a twenty eight year old with an accounting background became William's boss. William's former boss who was in his mid fifties, not yet eligible for early retirement was laid off. It turns out that most mid level supervisory, managerial administrative and professional employees who were over age forty with ten or more years service got caught up in the restructuring.

A few years earlier, the company had installed a very sophisticated truck routing system which made the loads and multiple deliveries efficient. The system featured an engineered labor standards (a system to measure productivity), that is the time it would take to make all of the deliveries. The system was very flexible in that it factored in traffic patterns at various times of the day and week. The system also allowed the company to give customers a fairly tight window of time when to expect to receive their deliveries. Until William started working for Geoff with few exceptions he met or exceeded the standards as set out by the system. The few exceptions were when traffic was unusually heavy or delays due to road closures. William and his coworkers felt the system was fair and it also allowed them to earn bonuses for meeting and exceeding the standards.

A few weeks after Geoff started he met with William to get to know him. Geoff asked William to go over his routine, which William did. "It's pretty basic really, I clock in, go to the dispatch office to get my schedule of deliveries, do a circle check of the truck for safety compliance, scan the bar code of each item to make sure that everything is accounted for and then I am on my way." Geoff asked how long this all took, to which Geoff replied that he could usually be on the road within half hour. "Isn't that a bit long?" asked Geoff to which William said "the system doesn't think so." Geoff said, "it is my understanding that the system is a guideline, and I think you should be able to cut it in half." William indicated he would try to see if he could do it quicker.

Geoff checked every day for the next two weeks and while William shaved off a few minutes it still averaged out to the half hour. Geoff met with William after the two weeks and said, "You are not trying very hard, are you," to which William replied, "I'm doing the best I can." Geoff became very agitated and indicated that he was going to keep a close eye on William and that he felt William was not measuring up to other drivers who exceeded the standards more often than he did.

After this confrontation William started having real difficulty in meeting the standards, at least three times per week for the next four weeks he ran over his schedule and the deliveries went beyond the tight window to the customer.

Every time this would happen Geoff would berate William often in front of the dispatcher and other drivers. After four weeks, William went to John, his union representative and indicated what was happening. John said, "William, if you are not meeting standards, they have the right to go after you."

The following week William was called in to a meeting with Geoff, John and a human resource person. William was given a written warning to improve his performance and unless his performance improved he could face further disciplinary action up to and including discharge.

Over the next number of weeks William pushed as hard as he could, took as many shortcuts as he could, stopped doing the circle check of his truck, went over the speed limits, hurried through each delivery, there was no time for any small talk with the customers and yet while there was improvement, there were still an unacceptable number of times he was not able to meet the standards.

During this time he noted that a number of other drivers were having the same difficulties; in fact, four had recently been fired for poor performance. William and some of his coworkers started to compare notes and discovered that all of the new hires had no trouble meeting the standards and most of the senior drivers were not. One of the senior drivers asked "do you think they are overriding the system?" The thought had occurred to William (drivers have a lot of time to think,) and he decided to meet with John again to lay out this possibility.

John indicated that he would request that the union's staff Industrial Engineer do an audit of the system. This occurred a week later and the Industrial Engineer validated that the system was fair and that it did not appear that it was being tampered with.

Over the next three months William was continually berated by Geoff and two more disciplinary meetings were held. At the second meeting Geoff indicated that unless there was significant improvement in the next two weeks, he would have no choice but to fire William. During this time frame six more senior driver's left, some were fired, others quit.

There was no significant improvement. John called William and advised him to resign and if he did not he would be fired and the union would not be able to protect him. He also pointed out that William would have far more difficulty in finding another job if he was fired. William submitted his resignation the next day giving two weeks' notice. Geoff accepted William's resignation and told him he would be paid for the two weeks but he did not have to come in.

All of this was not making sense to John and he kept thinking why none of the new hires were having difficulty and almost all of the senior drivers were. John then checked with the Industrial Engineer to make sure the system had integrity. The Industrial Engineer took great offence and said, "I told you it was; who are you to be questioning my professional ability?" John thought the response was a bit extreme, all he was doing was checking to be sure.

A few weeks later at a quarterly meeting held by the union, John relayed what was happening to the senior drivers at his location. Every other union representative John spoke to indicated the exact same thing was happening at their locations. "Remember after the last set of negotiations the company had a restructuring and they laid off people who had a lot of service?" one of the union representatives asked, adding, "Do you think that they are doing the same thing to the drivers?" Then it registered with John, thinking that with the two tier compensation structure it was certainly an incentive for the company to get rid of more senior people and if they got them to quit it was like winning to trifecta at a horse race, they avoided paying severance, reduced their average hourly rate and reduced their unfunded pension liability.

John with the help of union representatives at a number of other locations compiled a list of people who quit or were fired since the new agreement went into effect. They found that there was indeed a pattern, were 90 percent were over age forty with over ten years service. One of the representatives suggested to John that he approach one of the new supervisors brought in by the company who left shortly after joining. John was able to connect with him.

Fred was a twenty-six year old who after leaving the company worked for an automotive supply firm. Like Geoff, Fred had an accounting background. Fred initially was reluctant to speak with John, as when he left the company they insisted that he sign a confidentiality agreement and a breach of this could leave him open to a law suit. The head of Human Resources who conducted Fred's exit interview also implied that if Fred was to expose the company in any way he would be blacklisted for years. Although Fred was concerned about speaking to John, his conscience dictated that the story had to come out, too many people were having their lives' destroyed and it needed to be stopped. John and Fred met at a safe location and Fred relayed his experience.

Fred's first assignment was to learn the truck routing and standards system and then how to override the system. After three weeks of intensive one on one training he was assigned to a location and became a supervisor. Two weeks later his manager gave Fred a list of sixteen drivers that, in the manager's words, "were troublemakers and needed to be forced out of the company." The manager indicated that Fred's number one priority was to get them out. There was also a financial incentive involved, for every driver on the list who quit, Fred would receive a bonus of six thousand dollars and for every driver who was fired, three thousand, five hundred dollars. The reason for the difference is if the driver was fired, there would likely be severance involved.

The method to force the drivers out was to go into the system and alter the standard to the point where the targets would be impossible to achieve. The important thing was to phase this in for each driver on the target list so it would not be obvious. Once a trend of "not meeting standards" was established, Fred was to go after the driver and harass them to the point they quit. The manager indicated that the union's staff Industrial Engineer could do an audit of the system but not to worry as, "he is in our hip pocket."

Initially Fred played along, but after he realised that the driver's on the list were not the trouble makers the manager described but decent hard workers who were targeted in a systemic way so that the company could significantly reduce their labor costs. This was totally contrary to Fred's value system and he resigned.

Fred insisted on an exit interview with the Head of Human Resources and relayed the story to her. As indicated earlier Fred was warned to keep quiet.

John prepared a report and met with the President of the union. The staff Industrial Engineer was confronted and confessed that he was paid off by management to validate the integrity of the system. In exchange for a signed and witnessed affidavit he was allowed to resign which protected his retirement benefits.

A grievance was filed on behalf of every driver targeted, who either quit or was fired subsequent to the new collective agreement.

The union is also in discussions with other employee groups who were similarly targeted, to convince them to file a class action suit against the company. (as these groups were not represented by the union, they were unable to file a grievance.)

Predictably the company is denying any wrongdoing and vigorously fighting the grievance filed.

Case Study—Exploitation—Leila's Story

Leila never wanted to leave the Philippines. Married with two small children, she and her husband struggled financially to make ends meet. Leila, a nurse by training, and her husband, a construction worker, the found themselves in and out of the workforce, due to the countries high rate of unemployment and poverty. When they were both working, they barely made enough money to pay the rent on a small one bedroom apartment in Manila, let alone buy a house where the family could reside and raise their children properly.

Leila had a sister working as a nanny in Canada. When Leila found herself out of work for nearly six months, and her husband lost his job, she decided to apply to work abroad as well. It was a tough decision, for she knew she would be leaving her two small children, ages four and two. But she promised to write every day and return for visits every year. Leila knew from her sister and friends working in Canada that she could earn as much as $1,200 a month, three times as much as she earned in the Philippines. She would send all of her salary home to support her husband. Leila also discovered, during a training course to work as a caregiver in Canada, that after two years of employment, she could apply for Canadian permanent residency, essentially citizenship. She began to dream of offering her own children better lives, access to good Western schools and universities. She also dreamed of becoming a nurse in Canada when she completed the Live-in Caregiver Program (LCP). The

LCP states that a nanny must complete two years of full time employment within a three-year period. While in the LCP the caregiver must live in her employer's home.

It took six months for Leila to complete a required training program in Manila, which taught her basic care giving skills that she already knew from nursing. She then paid an employment agency the equivalent of $2000, which she borrowed from a bank, to find her a placement in Canada. Finally, her employer, a wealthy woman in Vancouver, British Columbia, agreed to sponsor Leila under the LCP to work as her nanny. The woman, Rita, had five children, ranging in age from four to sixteen. Leila would be responsible or so the letter of employment stated, for looking after the children, only.

Leila said her painful goodbyes and left for Canada. She arrived in Vancouver on an unusually snowy day in January. From the get go, Leila encountered one problem after another. Her employer didn't pick her up at the airport for nearly three hours. Leila waited in the terminal, impatiently pacing back and forth. The telephone number given to her by her employment agency didn't work. Leila had no way of reaching her new boss. When her new employer did arrive, she said she had to run some errands before taking Leila to the house. Leila, who was tired due to both the long flight and the time difference, was put to work right away, preparing a dinner for the entire family and cleaning up before she was able to even unpack.

Her days unfolded much the same. Leila was told she had to be up and working by 6am, preparing breakfasts and lunches for the children for school. The youngest, age 4, only attended kindergarten half a day, so Leila was responsible for caring for him in the mornings. After she walked the older children to school, she had to clean the dishes, do laundry, vacuum and clean the washrooms, all the while looking after the 4 year old. None of the children did chores and were not neat. Leila found herself cleaning up their rooms. She then had to make two dinners:

one for the children and another for her employers who ate later. Often she was not finished cleaning the dinner dishes and kitchen until nine or ten at night. Her employers also had dinner parties every week, at which Leila was told she had to cook and serve. Leila found herself working seven days a week, from about 6:00 am until 9:00 pm.

If this wasn't bad enough, Leila then learned that her employer was docking room and board from her salary. Leila would only be earning $600 a month. Leila's bedroom was a cot set up in the basement beside the furnace. She prayed to the whirl of the machine and in the damp winter months shivered under her blankets. There was no door to her room, so the children could come and go as they pleased. Leila was also not allowed to use the computer to email or call her family accept for Sunday mornings and only for one hour.

All the while, her female employer said she was one of the family and should make herself feel comfortable. But she wasn't allowed to eat with the family. She had to eat on her own and she was not allowed to buy her own food. She knew no one, accept a few nannies she began meeting at the park when she took the four year old. She felt lonely and isolated. One day, some of the Filipino nannies Leila was befriending at the park, told her to speak to her employer about having one day off a week, if not two and to reduce her hours so she could have evenings free to pray and knit, as she liked to make her children sweaters. Leila got the courage to do so. Her employer was furious, wanting to know with whom she was speaking who would advise her so poorly. Her employer took her passport and said that if she didn't do as she was told, Leila could return to the Philippines. She would put her back on the airplane but there was no way she was staying in Canada, unless she followed her rules. "I will have you deported," she screamed at Leila.

Leila was heartbroken. When she finally had a chance to call her husband, she broke down crying. But she couldn't tell him the truth as to why. She was homesick and feeling like she had made a big mistake. She told her husband, instead, that she just missed their children, but the job was going well. She didn't want him to worry about her

Leila's employer gave her more work to do than ever. Her employer would make lists of things she had to do during the day, including cleaning the silver ware, dropping clothes off at the dry cleaner, cleaning the fridge and doing the gardening. The family also had two dogs that Leila was now responsible for walking.

Then one day, Leila was in the kitchen and the four year old called her yellow skin. Leila was trying to get him to eat some carrots. He threw them at Leila's face and hissed: "You're not my mom. You can't tell me what to do. Go home, yellow skin." Leila got angry with the boy, and said that carrots were good for him to eat and that he should not call people names. The boy started wailing, alerting the attention of Leila's employer who came running. When she saw the child upset, she got mad at Leila. When Leila recounted what the child had said to her, her employer slapped her across the face. "How dare you accuse my son of being bad! Go to your room."

Leila's employer started docking her salary whenever anything on her list was not completed. Leila felt shy and insecure around all the children. She walked with her head down and kept her gaze to the floor. The once happy and upbeat young woman fell into a deep depression. She feared for her physical safety as her employer had her passport. She was overworked and tired.

The other nannies at the park recognized that Leila was being bullied and through several meetings, got her to open up about the emotional blackmail going on at the home. The training programs in the Philippines did not tell Leila she had legal rights in Canada, even under the Live-In Caregiver Program, including a locked room to sleep in, overtime pay and days off. Leila feared coming forward filing a complaint with immigration because her employer had her passport and said she would have her deported should she disobey any order. The nannies said this was also against the law. Leila, nonetheless, was too afraid to do anything. All she could think about was the better life she was giving her children through her salary and eventual residency in Canada.

But things in the home turned worse. One night, her male employer came into the furnace room drunk and tried to attack Leila. She fended him off by throwing her Bible at him. He was too drunk to protest and just passed out. The next day, however, her female employer fired her, saying that she had come on to her husband and that she was a slut. Leila had an hour to pack her things and find somewhere to go. On the way out the door, her employer returned the passport.

Luckily, Leila had the other nannies, and they referred her to an agency in Vancouver who helps live in caregivers in distress. Leila eventually found another job, with a good employer who pays her fairly, does not overwork her and does not threaten her with deportation. Leila discovered that most nannies in Canada are from the Philippines and that few know they have legal and human rights. Even if they do know, most are too afraid while under the program to file complaints against their employers. The LCP is ripe with abuse: from physical harassment to emotional blackmail. Many have called it modern day slavery, in which the workplace has moved from the business towers to the kitchens and living rooms, and many parents seem to take advantage of the power they have over these women from developing countries, desperate to earn incomes to support their families and provide better lives for their children. Leila was a broken woman after her first experience in Canada. But her story represents so many others.

Bullying and Stakeholders External To The Organization

Stakeholders other than employees are not immune from being bullied.

There are numerous reported incidences:

- In policing, brutality seems routine (the LAPD and RCMP being the most notorious).
- In nursing, patients being abused by healthcare providers and healthcare providers being bullied by patients and or the patients' family members.
- In education, teachers and professors seeking sexual favours in exchange for higher marks, and students and or parents bullying teachers in retaliation for not progressing or receiving lower marks.
- In retail and the service industry, customers bullying sales people.

As with employees, it is difficult to capture the true dimensions of the problem because the targets and bystanders are afraid to report. In policing, the use of cameras to record interactions between officers and citizens they apprehend is proving to be an effective deterrent.

In Dictatorial and Disjointed cultures, particularly if there are no appropriate checks and balances, Service Providers and Vendors are subject to bullying, usually under the rationalization that the buyer is just driving a hard bargain and is a tough negotiator and considered a hero. In organizations that have lax ethical standards, bully buyers prosper.

Case Study—Learning From the Parents—Toni's Story

Until June of 2009 Toni was a teacher at a Private School for girls. Toni was regarded as an exceptionally good teacher and received high scoring in her performance reviews and feedback from students in each of the five years she taught there. Prior to her posting at this school Toni spent eleven years in the public school system. Toni also has a Master's of Education degree.

In January of 2009 the parents of one of Toni's seventh grade students asked to meet with her. At the meeting the parents expressed their displeasure on how their daughter Julie was being graded. Toni indicated to the parents that while Julie definitely had the potential for higher grades, her attitude and not applying herself were holding her back. Julie's parents reacted badly to this and indicated that they would take the matter up with Margaret, the schools Head.

The next day Toni was called into Margaret's office. Margaret indicated that Julie's parents had lodged a complaint against her. The complaint was that Toni was unfair in the grading she gave Julie. They also indicated that Toni was very rude to them when they met. Toni gave Margaret her side of the story and indicated that she was very fair in the grades she gave, in that there was very little subjectivity. Margaret asked Toni to reassess, to which Toni responded that she would be happy to, conditional on Julie being retested in the subjects that she had scored low in. Margaret felt that this would be appropriate and advised the parents, who did not like the idea but agreed provided that Julie be given three weeks to study for the exams. Toni made the observation that giving Julie this kind of time to study for the retesting could have her falling behind in her current courses.

Three weeks later Julie took the exams and the grading was marginally better, also as Toni predicted Julie was falling behind in her current courses. The parents went back to Margaret and complained that Julie was set up for failure and Toni had made the re-examination tougher than the original tests, they also complained that Toni was retaliating against Julie by being harder on her than other students and that this was the reason Julie was falling further behind. Margaret supported Toni by indicating that Toni had warned them that Julie's falling behind could occur because her focus would be on the retesting at the expense of her current courses, and she also indicated that in the five years Toni had taught there, no complaints of this nature had ever been lodged.

For the next few weeks Margaret received at least one call a week from Julie's parents with complaints ranging from how Toni was treating Julie, ignoring her, to singling her out with the most difficult questions, making fun of her in front of other students and threatening to give her failing grades. Margaret went to Toni each and every time a complaint was made. Toni denied every allegation and asked Margaret to investigate by interviewing Julie and other students in the class. Margaret did this and found Julie to be very belligerent. In speaking to other students when asked "Does Ms. Allen single any students out for special treatment or punishment?" Every one indicated that they felt that Toni treated everyone the same and made a point of telling Margaret how much they liked Toni. One of the students mentioned that Julie had told her "my parents are going to get Ms Allen fired."

This validated for Margaret that Julie's parents were definitely out to get Toni. Margaret met with Richard, the long standing

Chair of the Board, about her concerns and asked him to intervene with Julie's parents. Richard indicated that he was uncomfortable doing this as the parents had already approached him on this and he felt that there was some merit to the concerns they had about Toni. Margaret was dumbfounded, and asked why he had not come to her. Richard responded by indicating he had questions regarding how she (Margaret) handled the situation and wanted to consult with other Board members before he approached her. "Well I expect that you will do this before the week is finished, because if you don't I will call a meeting with the entire Board so that I can relay to them what is going on. You are obviously taking Julie's and her parents' word on this over mine and I do not have the confidence that you will properly represent and support Toni and myself on this matter."

Richard did not expect this response and tried to backtrack by indicating that he had not formed a judgement but wanted advice from others before he proceeded further. "Well I don't understand why you did not come to me first," Margaret responded, adding, "We have a situation where Toni is being bullied by Julie and her parents and I want it stopped; that's why I came to you." Richard and Margaret agreed to meet early the next week to determine a course of action.

The following Monday, Richard and Margaret met, and Richard started by telling Margaret that Julie's family had a long history with the school and the parents were major donors. "I am well aware of this and I do not understand why that should have any bearing on the situation; it does not give them the licence to bully," Margaret interjected. "Well the Board does not share your view, in fact they agree with Julie's parents that Toni is the bully here," Richard replied.

Richard added that the Board had decided that Toni should be let go and directed Margaret to inform her. Margaret indicated that she disagreed with this decision and if the Board did not reconsider, she would view this as a lack of confidence in her and would view this as constructive dismissal. Richard then informed Margaret that he considered this insubordination and fired her.

Margaret went to Toni to indicate what was coming down. Toni thanked Margaret for standing up for her and was distressed that Margaret lost her position because of it. Margaret told Toni that it would have been impossible for her to stay. Both Margaret and Toni filed constructive dismissal suits and settled out of court for considerably more than they would have received under normal severance arrangements because the Board did not want to have this made public.

A new Head was recruited. Julie's new teacher was forced to fudge her grades. Richard and the Board are still in place.

Case Study—The Customer Is Always Right—Allen's Story

Allen was a Sales Associate in the Women's Department of a high end Department Store Chain. He joined them in January of 2010, after moving back to Toronto from New York City where he spent eleven years with a similar high end retailer.

In May of 2010 a customer, Ms Jones, bought an evening gown from Allen. While Ms Allen was on the customer data base as a frequent shopper, this was the first time Allen sold to her. After the sale, Nancy, another sales associate went to Allen and said "I'll bet you a drink that she returns the dress on Monday." Allen asked, "Why do you say that?," "Oh, she does it all the time, here and at other stores, when she has a fancy function to go to she "buys" a garment, wears it to the event, and returns it after, claiming either it is flawed, bad fit or didn't like it after she got home." Allen asked Nancy, "Why is she not flagged in the system?" Nancy indicated that the rumour has it that Ms Jones is well connected in the community and if there is any trouble she has the ability to convince other customers to boycott the store.

Sure enough, the following Monday Ms Jones returned the gown, claiming that the color just was not right for her. Allen indicated that he had to check with the Manager. Nigel, the manager was very familiar with Ms Jones and gave the approval for a credit. When Allen objected, Nigel said "don't fight it kid, that's the way it is" adding "remember one thing Allen, around here the customer is always right."

In giving Ms. Jones the credit Allen asked her how she enjoyed the event on Saturday night. In a haughty tone Ms. Jones asked, "What are you implying young man?" "Nothing really, my friends saw you there."

The next morning Allen was called into Nigel's office and told that Ms. Jones had called the owner of the store to complain that Allen had been impertinent. Allen told Nigel what he had said and observed that Ms. Jones obviously made the connection that he knew that she had worn the returned gown to the event. Nigel told Allen that the owner wanted Allen to send a note of apology with a one hundred dollar gift certificate (which would be deducted from his commission). Allen refused and was fired. Nigel did not like what he had to do and said, "I am sorry Allen, it is out of my hands and the owner is insistent."

Allen filed for wrongful dismissal and the case proceeded to discovery. Allen did his homework and found ten instances where Ms. Jones had made purchases of evening gowns over a two year period and made returns after she had worn them at events. He also had pictures that were in the society pages of the major newspaper, including the gown he had "sold" to her.

Allen's lawyer indicated to the store's lawyer that they intended on calling Ms. Jones as a witness. When the owner became aware of this she instructed the lawyer to do whatever it takes to settle. Allen received a handsome cash settlement and letters of apology from the owner and Ms. Jones (something that Allen insisted be part of the settlement).

How Big Is the Issue?

There has been a historical disregard for the seriousness of workplace bullying. The same was once true for domestic violence and schoolyard bullying, which are both recognised today as serious issues with grave consequences and that require intervention on multiple levels, including but not limited to legal remedies.

In the interviews conducted with organizational leaders (see "Organizational Leaders Don't Get It—Worse Yet They Don't Want To Get It"), most felt bullying in the workplace was no big deal. This view is not shared by the workers. Anecdotal evidence suggests that almost everyone (including the leaders interviewed) has in some way been impacted over the course of their careers.

People often find it difficult to talk publicly about workplace bullying and are afraid to report, which makes it hard to capture the true dimensions of the problem. As in other abusive relationships, at first, targets often deny, minimize, or trivialize the abuse as a way to survive it; and the bullies minimize, rationalize, or excuse their behavior or blame the target. For the target, the major risk in admitting to being harassed at work is that it can have a stigmatizing effect where others might see it as a weakness or an inability to cope. In health care, nurses are conditioned to believe that being harassed and abused by patients goes with the territory.

In a survey done in 2009 by Curtin University of Technology in Perth, Australia, Rose Chapman, PhD and her colleagues reported that 92 percent of the nurses at one hospital reported they had been verbally abused, 52 percent physically assaulted, and 69 percent threatened with violence. Half mentioned the incidents to their supervisors or coworkers but only 16 percent filed a formal report. Over the course of the year, forty-two official reports had been filed, but in 95 percent of those cases, "the only action taken by the hospital was making staff in the area aware of the incident. No other actions had been documented." Almost one third of those who were part of the survey said they didn't report workplace violence because it "happens all the time and is simply part of the job."

European research into the problem began in the early 1980s in Scandinavian countries and spread during the late 1990s to other European countries, Australia, New Zealand, and Asia.

It was through the work of Loraleigh Keaschly (Wayne State University, Detroit, MI) in the 1990s that a conceptual framework for workplace bullying emerged in the United States. Prior to this there has been very little research in English on the topic.

The Workplace Bullying Institute commissioned one of the largest surveys on the topic in 2007. Zogby International (located in Utica, NY was founded by John Zogby) conducted 7,740 online interviews of a random sample that is representative of the population of the United States. The survey found that nearly half of American adults have either been bullied at work or been a witness. According to this data, incidences of bullying are four times more prevalent than all illegal forms of harassment. In 62 percent of cases where abuse was reported to an employer, the employer did nothing or made the problem worse by retaliating against the target. Only 3 percent of those who were bullied filed lawsuits, 40 percent never complained at all. For 77 percent of the targets, the only way they could stop the bullying was to leave their employment

To determine the effect of the economic downturn on bullying, the Namie's did a further follow-up in 2009, entitled "Still Bullying With Impunity." The research question was: "Are bullies being swept up in layoffs more than bullied targets?" The study concluded that: "Bullies are not losing their jobs during the recession and are not being purged. Targets are still banished from employment, while bullies still abuse with impunity." In fact, 27 percent of the respondents reported that the bullying got worse during the economic downturn.

In 2010, Workplace Bullying Institute developed a second scientific survey commissioned through Zogby International and found the results were essentially unchanged from 2007.

According to the UK's, The Daily Telegraph, a 2010 UK, an online poll of ten thousand people found that 92 percent believe they are the target of workplace taunts and intimidation, with 56 percent believing it is a serious problem in their office, shop or factory. It is also found that just under 50 percent blame their immediate manager for bullying them, while a similar proportion claimed their complaints were not properly dealt with.

Another UK study found that 53 percent had been bullied at work and 78 percent witnessed bullying at work.

The 2010 UK poll indicated that 51 percent of the British workforce are on the hunt for a new job, the top reason is a "feud" with a boss or coworker, according to 53 percent of the 2,000 respondents.

Based on the research done to date it is reasonable to believe that the majority of employees, at some time during their career, will be exposed to systematic bullying or other forms of abusive behaviour either directly or indirectly.

Costs, Liabilities And Deadly Consequences

> "Workplace bullying—in any form—is bad for business. It destroys teamwork, commitment and morale."
>
> —Tony Morgan, Chief Executive, The Industrial Society

In 'The Cost Of Bad Behavior: How Incivility is Damaging Your Business and What To Do About It, Christine Porath, Ph.D., from the University of Southern California indicated, time wasted at work or spent searching for another job could cost companies up to 300 billion dollars a year. Further, the American Institute of Stress (AIS) estimates that one million workers are absent each workday in the USA due to stress. The Institute calculated that it costs companies $300 billion a year in absenteeism, health expenses, and programs to help workers manage stress. This estimate does not include the cost of reduced productivity due to lowered morale, recruitment and training costs for new hires, stress related workman's comp claims, bad press, or litigation.

In a poll of 800 managers and employees in seventeen industries Christine Porath and her associate Christine Pearson found:

"Among workers who've been on the receiving end of incivility:

- 48 percent intentionally decreased their work effort.
- 47 percent intentionally decreased the time spent at work.
- 38 percent intentionally decreased the quality of their work.
- 80 percent lost work time worrying about the incident.

- 63 percent lost work time avoiding the offender.
- 66 percent said that their performance declined.
- 78 percent said that their commitment to the organization declined.
- 12 percent said that they left their job because of the uncivil treatment.
- 25 percent admitted to taking their frustrations out on customers."

Successful lawsuits have cost companies and institutions millions, a few examples are:

- One of the largest amount yet obtained for a single person in a racial discrimination case in the United States was $2.5 million paid by Lockheed Martin in January of 2008 to Charles Daniels, a former avionics electrician who was targeted for over a year on a daily basis by coworkers and a supervisor with racial slurs and threats, including threats of violence after he filed a complaint. Following the internal zero tolerance complaint procedures, he was not only not protected from retaliation, the abuse escalated and his work was sabotaged. Commenting on the settlement, he said, "I was subjected to constant racial slurs, harassment, threats of violence and retaliation, which left me afraid of my safety, depressed, humiliated and subjected to reprisals. I am grateful to be able to put this case to rest, even if the memories of what occurred are still fresh in my mind.
- In 2006 FedEx lost a lawsuit filed by two employees who were awarded 61 million dollars in punitive and compensatory damages for creating a hostile work environment causing emotional distress and failing to enforce its anti-discrimination policies. This case has also put individual managers on high alert, since part of the

compensatory damages included a manager at FedEx having to personally pay 1 million dollars. This was awarded under a California law allowing individuals to be held personally liable for workplace harassment.

- In 2010 a North Carolina company paid $230,000 to settle a lawsuit on behalf of a factory worker who was viciously assaulted by her plant manager after the worker reported the manager's sexual harassment to company officials.

- The Ashland School District in Wisconsin paid $900,000.00 to Jamie Nabozay, who was subjected to homophobic slurs and repeated vicious assaults by his peers and adults in the district. The administrators failed to respond to the numerous complaints against his perpetrators and at times vigorously defended the bullies and blamed Jamie for the violence. The movie, "Bullied: a Student, a School, and a Case That Made History" documented the case.

- In 2010 Arkansas-based Superior Forestry Service, Inc. agreed to pay $2.75 million in a Southern Poverty Law Center lawsuit on behalf of guest workers who were systematically cheated and abused.

- In 2006, Officer Nancy Sulz, a $50,000 police officer with eight year experience won nearly $1 million from the Royal Mounted Police for being bullied by a senior officer.

- In 2011, a case against the National Gallery of Victoria in Australia and its now former head of the gallery's commercial operations, Andrew O'Brien, was settled. Since a confidentiality agreement was signed the actual payout is unknown. The NGV is facing another bullying complaint against another gallery manager.

Although difficult to calculate, brand and reputation value has to take a hit in instances where violence in the workplace is exposed in the media. Consider what Rutgers University is experiencing after the video exposing bullying exploded in the media.

⁂

And the costs are more than just financial.

In the United States, an average of fifteen to twenty people are murdered weekly while at work. According to the U.S. National Institute for Occupational Safety and Health, homicide in the workplace is the fastest growing form of murder. Homicide is the leading cause of on-the-job death for women and the second leading cause for men. A further one million people are physically assaulted in the workplace every year, and even more are subjected to verbal violence. According to the US Dept. of Justice, BJS, 7/28/98 the workplace is the most dangerous place to be in America. The problem is so pervasive that the Center for Disease Control has classified workplace violence as a national epidemic.

A recent example is Christopher Dorner, the former LAPD officer, who is alleged to have killed four people and targeting as many as fifty other officers and their families in revenge for his 2008 firing. His act of terrorism ended in a barrage of bullets and a blazing fire in a cabin in California's San Bernadino Mountains on February 12, 2013. There is now an investigation in response to suggestions that Dormer was bullied by officers he targeted and blamed for his being fired.

In South Korea after a series of events, one involving a bullied marine corporal, who went on a shooting rampage killing four marines and wounding another, and a number of suicides, where bullying was a factor, a military culture of bullying and beating is drawing scrutiny by the Government and Korea's Defense Ministry.

On August 25, 2010, Michael Enright was charged with attempted murder and assault as a hate crime and possession of a weapon after he allegedly slashed a taxi driver's face and neck after Enright found out the driver was Muslim.

On March 11, 2011 Brittany Norwood allegedly killed her coworker, Jane Murray, at a Bethesda Maryland athletic apparel store. To cover her crime, she claimed that they were both attacked and sexually assaulted by two masked men. Norwood was arrested on March 18 and charged with first-degree murder.

On April 27, 2011 the lead air traffic controller was stabbed to death in the control tower of the Bale-Mulhouse airport in Saint Louis, France. His alleged murderer is a coworker.

※

A United Nations report in 1996 estimated that worldwide, between 500,000 and 1.2 million people commit suicide every year (UN 1996). Real suicide rates are estimated to be 50-60 percent higher due to the stigma associated with reporting the deaths as such. Death by suicide exceeds the death toll of traffic accidents. While there is very little research to date on specific links of suicides or attempted suicides due to workplace bullying, there can be little doubt that it is a contributing factor when we consider that bullying is one of the main contributing or substantive factors in the suicide of children and young adults.

On July 30, 2010 Kevin Morrissey managing editor at the University of Virginia literacy magazine Virginia Quarterly Review, shot himself. Warnings and red flags to university officials by coworkers and Morrissey's sister went unheeded. It was reported that Morrissey placed at least eighteen calls to university officials in the final two weeks of his life.

In France there is an ongoing criminal investigation into allegations that management practices at France Telecom led several employees to commit suicide in recent years. The suicide rate at the telecommunications giant exceeds the national average. The probe is looking into a single case and will determine whether France Telecom and one of its managers could be brought to trial for involuntary homicide. This case is bringing forward the possible and perhaps probable connection between workplace bullying and suicide. In July of 2012, authorities placed the former head of France Telecom, Didier Lombard, under formal investigation regarding this and he is currently out on 100,000 euro bail.

※

Gavin de Becker of Gavin de Becker & Associates, Inc of Studio City, California, noted that people "at risk of committing terrible violence don't necessarily have a history of getting into trouble." This is especially true of people who are the target of a bully. When life seems intolerable—thanks in large part to rejection and humiliation—add SAD (sullen, angry and depressed), mix with media provocation and access to a weapon—and you have a Jonathan Russell, a "quiet man beset by personal woes," facing disciplinary action at work, who walked into his station on the soldering line and shot dead three coworkers and wounded another five before killing himself in Jefferson City, Mo. The reasons for acts of violence are as complex as the people who carry them out. However, keeping people from becoming targets of bullying could substantially reduce the number of workers chose death over the brutality of his coworkers and boss.

The Workplace As A Battlefield—
Workplace Bullying and PTSD

What people go through when they are bullied. In an interview with ABC News' reporter Radha Chitale, Laney College Professor William Lepowsky described how he felt while he was being ruthlessly targeted by his boss: "I was like a soldier crouched in a foxhole while shells were exploding around you...my world went from ordered, sensible and predictable to a nonsense 'Alice in Wonderland' world of insanity."

The German Psychotherapist, Dr. Heinz Leymann, found that people who had been relentlessly bullied at work suffered more intense and persistent Post Traumatic Stress Disorder (PTSD) than train conductors who witnessed suicides by people throwing themselves in front of the train. He discovered that PTSD is probably the correct psychiatric and psychological diagnosis for an astounding 95 percent of the targets of bullying. In an article in the European Journal of Work and Organizational Psychology, Dr. Leymann and Annelie Gustafsson found the train operators symptoms to be "very much milder" than all of the targets in their workplace bullying study. Also, the proportion of these train drivers who suffer PTSD and share the severe diagnosis was much smaller. In fact, the authors found that the reactions of targets of bullying compare more closely with a Norwegian study concerning raped women.

The core elements of PTSD include captivity or entrapment, psychological fragmentation, the loss of a sense of safety, trust, and self worth, as well as the tendency to be re-victimized. It is not difficult to see how these elements are at play in the workplace. There is certainly a sense of captivity or entrapment because people are usually dependent on their employment for their livelihood. Many adults spend more time at work than they do with their families, or sleeping, so it is understandable that the psychological impact of being bullied includes the loss of a sense of safety, trust and self worth. Usually workplace bullying is repeated and ongoing, which stands to reason that the target goes through the sense of re-victimization, because they are being re-targeted. And if the organization handles the situation poorly, they will once again be re-targeted.

Leymann points out that the train drivers did not experience a series of ongoing further traumatizing rights violations or identity insults from different societal sources such as the raped women and bullied employees. "Mobbing [bullying] and expulsion from the labor market are in themselves a series of victimizations of traumatic strength…torn out of their social network, a life of early retirement with permanent psychological damage threatens the great majority of mobbing victims." They found that many of the targets of bullying experienced mental effects fully comparable with PTSD from war or prison camp experiences.

A number of serious health conditions, both psychological and physical can accompany PTSD:

- depression
- obsession
- agitation
- blockage of the memory of the events
- a resigned attitude
- moderate cognitive disturbances
- automatically recurring thoughts

- irritability
- inner unrest
- panic/anxiety attacks
- hyposomnia
- addiction
- suicidal ideation, thoughts, plans, and attempts
- gastro-intestinal disturbances
- muscular disorders
- chronic muscle hypertension

Given these symptoms, it is no small wonder that the performance of people who are targeted deteriorates and they are viewed as having a poor attitude and insubordinate. Not only do they suffer the symptoms of PTSD, they offer the bully an excuse to continue to target them.

While there are presently no quantitative studies measuring the relationship between divorce and PTSD as a result of bullying, from the abundant anecdotal data available it is clear that marital breakdown is often one of the casualties of being bullied. Thus the target is even more alone with even less of a support structure, and more of the guilt and hurt.

Case Study—A Father's Confession—Tim's Story

In 2010 Tim's Dad Fred called him to come to his place as soon as possible. "I don't have much time left and I have a confession to make before I go," was his sombre plea.

At twenty-five Tim was the eldest of Fred's three children. Fred left his wife Mary eight years before and lived with his elderly mother who was the only person who would have him. Fred was an unemployed alcoholic and he had very little contact with his family in the eight years since he left. Tim recalls Fred's drinking problem started around ten years ago when Tim was fifteen and suspected that it was related to Fred being fired from his position as CFO of a Canadian retailer in 1998. In the few years before he left Fred was verbally and physically abusive to everyone in the family.

While Tim was civil whenever he had contact with Fred, he resented him for leaving and he considered Fred a looser. Andrea and Jim, Tim's brother and sister were more charitable in their feelings towards Fred, as was Mary, she regularly sent Fred's mother a cheque to help her out with the expenses as she knew Fred had no income and her mother in-law was not in a financial position to support him.

Fred was in a lot of pain; Tim could tell when they met. Fred told Tim the whole story which by the time he was finished Tim, who considered his dad to be a looser, now felt both outrage and regret. Outrage for what happened to his Dad and regret on how he treated and misjudged him.

Fred joined the Company in 1987 as a Comptroller and was promoted to CFO in 1996 reporting to Janice the CEO. Janice was a very demanding boss, but because of his performance and capabilities Fred did not suffer the abuse Janice doled out on a regular basis to others in the organization.

In August of 1997 Fred was offered a CFO position with a larger retailer. When he advised Janice he was leaving, she begged him to reconsider, giving him a huge raise, a staying bonus and a promise that he would be considered for her replacement in a few years time. Fred reconsidered and decided to stay.

A month after he decided to stay, Janice started to ride Fred, criticising almost everything that he did. The emails from Janice were endless, every day, at all hours, weekends and holidays. Everything was ASAP and Janice expected immediate responses, and if he did not respond immediately, she would send another. Janice started excluding Fred from critical meetings, did not communicate decisions she had made and started dealing directly with one of Fred's subordinates without involving him.

All of this started to erode Fred's confidence and as a result his performance. He did not know how to handle the situation. This is when he started to drink heavily which led to the downward spiral. As a result of the stress and the drinking, Fred gained weight and started having heart problems.

The harassment and abuse lasted eleven months. In August of 1999, exactly a year after Fred told Janice he was leaving, Janice fired Fred "for cause," citing his poor performance over the last year. Her parting comment was, "Nobody quits on me!"

Fred sought legal advice and the lawyer indicated to him that Janice had built up a very good case for terminating him and advised him to accept the three months severance that Janice had offered. Feeling he had no choice Fred accepted the offer.

Totally broken, unfit, and an alcoholic, Fred was not able to find new employment. He also found out that Janice had spread the word in the industry the reasons she fired him, he was blacklisted.

Having told the story to Tim, Fred felt a great relief.

It was the first time he had confided to anyone about what he had gone through, because he was ashamed. His health had deteriorated to the point that he had only weeks to live and he wanted to make things right and confess and apologise to his family, and chose Tim as the conduit.

Author's note

Fred passed away five weeks later. Believing he was at fault rather than the victim was the major reason for his downfall, which happens with all too many targets. There is no question that Fred suffered from PTST, and if he had not dealt with what he went through alone, or those who were close to him recognized the symptoms and intervened, Fred would be alive today.

I can clearly relate to what Fred went through as I was bullied and retailed against because I blew the whistle and exposed a corrupt executive.

While I am unable to relate my story—in my case I am bound by a nondisclosure agreement—I am able to tell the stories of others like Fred who had been negatively impacted because of bullying in the work place.

For me the experience was physically and emotionally debilitating. Also, for too long I was made to believe that I was the culprit; my self-confidence was destroyed and my relationship with family, friends, and associates were severely tested. I fell into what I call the *"The Bully's Trap,"* which, I have discovered, is all too common with people who are targeted.

Part Three

Effectively Dealing With The Issue

"Knowing what's right doesn't mean much unless you do what's right"

—Theodore Roosevelt

The Barriers

The 1999 International Labor Organization report on workplace violence stated that workplace violence is one of the most serious problems societies throughout the world face today. A major component of that violence is bullying. Many people report to work every day filled with fear and trepidation; others feign illness to avoid the relentless attacks; still others make themselves physically ill anticipating the inevitable harassment at the water cooler, out in the field, on the shop floor, or in the board room. People who are targeted spend a lot of time thinking of ways to avoid the trauma and have little energy left to do their job at all, let alone to do it well.

It is not only the person who is targeted who suffers the consequences of the bullying. Many people who do the bullying carry these supposedly "effective management tools" over into other parts of their lives—bullying their children, failing at interpersonal relationships, losing jobs and for some, like Jeffery Skilling of Enron, end up in jail.

Bystanders are also affected by the bullying. These onlookers may observe the bullying and merely turn a blind eye, walk away, jump in as accomplices, or actively intervene and help the targeted worker.

Stopping the bullying involves more than merely identifying and stopping the bully or offering counselling for the target. It requires that we examine the cultural climate of the organization that may be cultivating the bully, reinforcing the corrupting behavior of not-so-innocent bystanders, undermining the target of the bully, and making it difficult for witnesses, resisters and defenders to stand up for the targeted individual and speak out against the injustice.

There are five main obstacles to stopping this bullying:

1. Fear—Bullying is rarely reported by either the bullied or the bystander.

    - Those who do report are usually labelled "disgruntled employees" or "trouble makers", and are discredited and retaliated against.
    - Those who leave the organization because of bullying and/or whistle blowing often find they are blacklisted and have difficulty finding alternate employment.

2. Ignorance and Apathy

    - Ignorance: to not know what bullying is, what roles people play, and what needs to be done to address the issues effectively.
    - Apathy: to not care about the person who is targeted by the bully, or to not care that it is happening in the workplace is an even greater impediment than not knowing. Ignorance can be remedied through thoughtful and effective instruction. Not caring is far harder to fix.

3. The Attitudes and Behaviors of Leaders

    - CEO is also the CBO (Chief Bullying Officer)—Bosses are the bullies in over 70 percent of the reported incidents.
    - Leaders who do not view verbal or psychological abuse as violence or do not make the connection that

these types of predatory aggression can give rise to the physical aggression.

- Leaders who like bullies because they believe bullies get things done and are high performers. In many situations the CEO is also the CBO (Chief Bullying Officer.)

- Leaders who think employees will abuse workplace violence—harassment legislation, policies and procedures. They fear that any intervention to correct deficiencies will be considered harassment. In 2010 Michael Bloomberg, the Mayor of New York City warned that if the State of New York passed proposed legislation, many companies will move their work to New Jersey. He as much said: "If we don't allow companies to abuse employees, they will be uncompetitive!"

4. Organizational Response

- Ignoring the problem or retaliating against the target. In the majority of cases where abuse was reported to the employer, the employer ignored the problem or made the problem worse by retaliating against the target.

- Labeling a bullying situation as a personality clash, or an aggressive management style.

- Applying conflict resolution techniques which makes the situation worse for the target.

5. Governance

- Boards of Directors that do not monitor or audit cultural factors of an organization or have appropriate checks and balances in place to predict and identify bullying.

Many jurisdictions have workplace violence—and/or harassment legislation. Where there is legislation it is estimated that there is a 30 percent compliance rate. Some organizations that put policies, procedures and programs in place do so to be legally compliant, not necessarily to stop the bullying.

Workplace bullying and serious organizational problems go hand in hand.

In my experience, where bullying occurs, the following dynamics are usually at play:

- Leaders are more feared than respected by their employees.
- Fear is used as a substitute for motivation and positive leadership.
- There is a disproportionate focus on the short term, at the expense of sustainable long term performance.
- Leaders take massive risks with disregard for consequences.
- Leaders condone lax ethical standards such as inflated reporting, affairs, kickbacks.
- People are considered expendable.
- There is subjectivity and ambiguity in performance management and advancement.
- Individual performance is rewarded over team performance.
- There are few checks and balances to prevent or stop wrong doing.
- Contrary viewpoints or opinions are not welcome.
- There is failure at the governance level to intervene effectively when bullying is reported.

As I have asserted in Part One, workplace bullying is part of a larger systemic issue that requires a systemic change. For bullying to stop, it requires a cultural change that is culturally and organizationally centered.

Andrew Faas

Bullying and the Attraction and Retention of Talent

Attraction and retention of talent will become the biggest catalyst for organizations to ensure that their workplaces are safe and free from bullying.

I have worked with a number of companies in a variety of sectors across North America on cultural transformation. For many, what triggered the initiative, was the ability to attract and retain talent, many wanted to build on cultures to establish themselves as the organization of choice, for both customers and employees. One bank I worked with has as their number one initiative establishing the firm as the firm of choice for women with wealth and women in wealth.

Within five years, the attraction and retention of talent will emerge as the biggest challenge for employers. This is already the case in some sectors, health care and technology, as examples.

Notwithstanding the current levels of unemployment, demographics dictate that the participation rate will decrease at a greater rate than the demand for employees in most sectors and categories of employees.

In addition to the lower participation rate, research is showing that the defection rate will dramatically rise. A 2010 survey of British workers, indicates that an astounding 50 percent want to leave their current organization when the economy turns around—the main reason, conflict with their boss or coworker (read bullying.) Realistically not all of the 50 percent are going to defect, but the extent of the discontent is disturbing.

One organization I worked with, had great difficulty convincing search firms to recruit for them because the organization had a terrible reputation, where bullying was not only condoned, it was encouraged.

As part of the cultural transformation process, I encourage organizations to develop a Value Exchange Model (based on the Ethic of Reciprocity) with the various employee categories. In retail the Value Exchange Model with customers is widely used by the tier one retailers. This model is understanding and delivering on the expectations that each have of each other.

Factoring Bullying into the Being Hired / Hiring Equation

Given that there will be more choices for people when they decide to change employment, the cultures of prospective employers will become a major factor.

In making a decision whether to change employers, I encourage people to conduct a thorough due diligence, and avoid going from a known situation to one that is an unknown and potentially toxic. In "Pam's Story—Onto Pleasure Island" I relay what happened to Pam when she left a positive situation after nine successful years and found herself in a totally toxic one. Had Pam done better due diligence she could have avoided what became a living nightmare that continues to haunt her.

When considering a change I recommend the following:

1. *Understand what you are leaving.*

    For over 70 percent of those who are bullied, the only way to stop the bullying is quit. You do not have to quit to have the bullying stop, and if this is the main or only reason, you should consider your options.

2. *Have the search firm/recruiter consider you an equal client.*

The search firm/recruiter has the inside knowledge of the organization and should be able to answer questions regarding the culture and history of the organization and its people.

While the organization is the paying client, potential and successful candidates must be considered equal as clients. Part of what they must do is properly and honestly make people aware of what they are getting into, and be held accountable if they misrepresent the situation and, as in Pam's case, it does not work out, being able to seek legal recourse.

3. *Find out as much as you can about the organization.*

Talk to people you know in the organization. If you don't know anyone, as part of the recruitment process ask to have access to two or three people who will give candid input. Being able to speak to the person you are replacing will provide valuable insight. If you know former employees of the organization, they will likely be more comfortable being candid.

Check the net for any media reports related to bullying/violence, sexual harassment, human rights claims, class action lawsuits, reported or alleged wrongdoings, and union certification drives.

Talk to people external to the organization. Vendors and clients you may know will have insights and viewpoints that can help you assess.

4. *Questions you should be asking.*

- What are the values and operating principles, and how are they applied?
- What are the characteristics of the culture in the organization? (See section "What's Culture Got To Do With It.")

- Who am I replacing? And if that person left, how long was she with the organization and in the position and why did she leave?
- What is the turnover rate in the organization and the department?
- Are exit interviews conducted? What are the reasons people cited for leaving?
- Why is this an external hire?
- As part of the hiring and advancement to management processes, are psychological assessments conducted? (If the answer to this one is no—beware!)
- What is the investment in management and leadership training?
- Do regions and/or departments operate on an integrated basis or as silos?
- Describe the performance management system. What gets measured? What's the balance between individual and team? To what extent are performance reviews two way discussions?
- Do terms of engagement exist for resolving differences and disputes?
- Are there policies, procedures and practices in place relating to code of conduct and conflict of interest?
- What are the highlights of the latest employee attitude/engagement survey? What was the participation rate in the latest survey?
- Is employee absenteeism a problem?
- What did the organization do to minimize the negative impact on people during the economic downturn?
- Are contrarian viewpoints welcome?

- In terms of organizational priorities, where does talent rank? In the annual plan what are the specific initiatives in place that focus on talent as a priority?

5. *Find out as much as you can about the person you will be reporting to.*

    - "Tenure with the organization and in the position
    - Style
    - Personality
    - Any history of harassment or bullying
    - Relationship with people in the department
    - Relationship with the person you are replacing"

    In assessing the organizations culture, try to connect all of the information and look for any inconstancies. If there are inconsistencies, seek clarification.

6. *Be honest about why you are making the change.*

    You will be asked why you are making a change.

    If the reason you are leaving your current employer is to stop the bullying, you don't have to get into the gory details, you can simply state that your values do not align with those of the organization.

Attraction and retention of talent should be one of the top priorities in every organization. The culture of the organization, or put another way, what the organization stands for and how it operates is the biggest factor in why people decide to join and stay.

In the event you run into resistance, receive vague responses, or there are inconsistencies in the responses, consider these to be indicators of the culture that exists. The recruiter in enticing you to join will try to sell, and understandably accentuate the positive. If you are informed, you will be able to determine if what is portrayed is either real or not.

I also advise you to take notes of all of the conversations you have during the hiring process. This record will help you seek recourse, if there has been a misrepresentation and the move ends badly.

Is There a Psychopath in the House?

As with most issues there is rarely a magic bullet to resolve the problem. Bullying in the workplace is no exception. As I have previously stated to stop bullying from occurring it takes a comprehensive, integrated approach. There is one thing however that comes close to being a magic bullet, which is for organizations to make mandatory a psychological test for anyone who is being hired or promoted to a management or supervisory position.

A highly regarded psychologist Robert Hare developed a checklist of twenty telltale signs that helps detect whether someone is a psychopath—being a predator who uses charm, manipulation, intimidation, sex and violence to control others and to satisfy their own selfish needs. This description matches many of the bullies that I have profiled. Hare is convinced many important CEOs and politicians fall into this category.

The twenty telltale signs devised by Hare are as follows:

- "glib and superficial charm
- grandiose (exaggeratedly high) estimation of self
- need for stimulation
- pathological lying
- cunning and manipulative
- lack of remorse or guilt
- shallow affect (superficial emotional responsiveness)

- callousness and lack of empathy
- parasitic lifestyle
- poor behavioral controls
- sexual promiscuity
- early behavioral problems
- lack of realistic long term goals
- impulsivity
- failure to accept responsibility for own actions
- many short-term marital relationships
- juvenile delinquency
- revocation of conditional release
- criminal versatility"

Organizations should rely on professionals like industrial psychologists to make the assessments.

Case Study—I Flunked The Test And They Still Hired Me!—Andrew's story

One company, a conglomerate of a number of related business units, I worked with has had a psychological assessment part of their hiring and advancement protocol for over two decades. This company had the characteristics of a Stable culture. The CEO decided to retire after a very successful twelve years run as CEO. The selection committee of the board established the criteria for the new CEO and they placed a heavy emphasis on bringing in a change agent, someone who had the experience and background to reinvent the company. While the company was very successful in the past, market conditions and new competition threatened the sustainability of revenue and earnings growth.

After an extensive and long international search process, the search committee identified an individual who looked like a perfect match to the profile established. On paper Andrew was by far the most qualified of any of the other candidates, he interviewed well and he was a recognized change agent having turned around three major organizations in the last fifteen years. As is the case when attracting someone away from other organization, it was difficult to obtain direct references. Those that the executive recruiter was able to get were positive, particularly regarding Andrew's background and experience. One common theme however was that Andrew was very demanding and "does not suffer fools lightly."

When Andrew was told that he had to go through a psychological assessment before an offer was made, he reacted by indicating that he viewed this as insulting and threatened to withdraw from the running. The executive recruiter after much persuasion convinced Andrew to have the assessment done, indicating to him that this was a long standing protocol, and there were no exemptions. Andrew was also told not to worry about it, it was just a process that the head of human resources insisted on, and the selection committee had already made up their mind, regardless of the results of the assessment.

John, an industrial psychologist has been doing the testing and interviews with candidates for management positions with the company for the last seven years, with an incredible track record. The company only hired or promoted people who John felt would be successful in the culture. The management team were considered to be the best and the brightest in the industry. Turnover of staff was very low. On the annual engagement surveys, the scores for leadership, communication and being treated with respect were always higher than the benchmark of other companies. The performance and productivity metrics over the last ten years exceeded those of benchmark companies in the industry, worldwide.

When John administered the test and interviewed Andrew he knew almost from the outset that Andrew would not be a good fit. While Andrew was obviously on his best behavior during the interviews, with John he was defensive, mocked the process and declared "When I become the CEO, you won't be doing much work with us". The assessment concluded that Andrew was close to being a psychopath.

John presented his findings to the head of human resources, the chair of the selection committee and the executive recruiter. Both the executive recruiter and the head of the selection committee rejected John's assessment. The executive recruiter discredited John by indicating he had a reputation in the industry for not being objective and did not like people who were demanding and tough. The head of human resources argued that John's track record was solid. The chair of the selection committee argued that the criteria they had established called for a change agent and "to make the changes that need to be done, we need one tough bastard". At the insistence of the head of human resources John's report was submitted to the selection committee and then to the full board.

The board was clearly divided, most felt uncomfortable in making an offer given the report, however the head of the selection committee made a strong argument citing the need for "one tough bastard", he also reminded them that there was no strong alternative and that the board was under tremendous pressure from shareholders to name a CEO. After much debate a decision was make to make an offer to Andrew, which he accepted. No reference to the assessment was made.

What John outlined in his report, proved to be accurate. According to the head of human resources, Andrew's behavior was far worse than what he anticipated, knowing what was in the report. Within one year from Andrew's date of hire the culture went from Stable to Dictatorial. Eight of the twelve members of the senior management team resigned, including the head of human resources. Andrew brought in people (all male) that worked for him at his previous companies to replace those who left. They became Andrew's henchmen. Relationships with employees and vendors deteriorated. Fault lines were starting to show, all of the performance metrics were on a downward trend. Andrew tried to force the CFO to report inflated revenue and profit numbers. The CFO refused and Andrew fired her for insubordination. She was given a huge severance, with the understanding that she would not reveal to anyone the events surrounding her termination. The board was clueless as to what was going on.

Two years into his tenure, Andrew knew that he could only hide the inevitable for so long, so he decided that rather than reinvent the company and grow it, the better option was to divest any part that was not core. The board bought into this strategy and 80 percent of the business was sold for what most who knew what the potential was, at too low a multiple. The board considered Andrew a hero for avoiding what they thought was a potential long term disaster, and gave him a multi-million dollar incentive for successfully dismantling the company. Andrew also triggered the change of control provision in his agreement (which stipulated that if over 50 percent of the company were sold, a multi-million dollar severance would be paid).

All of the businesses that were sold, turned into great acquisitions and solid performers, validating what those in the know were representing—that they were sold at too low a multiple.

Author's Note

Andrew went on to become CEO of another major organization whose performance started to significantly deteriorate a year and a half after Andrew became it's "leader."
The decline and fall of this company could have been avoided had the board taken the psychological assessment seriously.

Again over 70 percent of bullying is boss to subordinate. By not hiring or promoting a bully to a position of power reduces the risk of bullying. Having a scientifically proven method to identify bullies is as close to a magic bullet to stop bullying from occurring and I highly recommend that all organizations make a psychological assessment part of their hiring for and promotion to management protocol.

Part Four

Guidance and Advice

"Never give in, never give in, never, never, never, never—in nothing, great or small in except to conviction of honour and good sense never yield to force: never yield to the apparently overwhelming might of the enemy."

—Winston Churchill

Overcoming It— Advice to The Bullied

> "Although the world is full of suffering, it is full also of the overcoming of it."
>
> —Helen Keller

In most cases of bullying in the workplace, people allow it to happen, do not report it and try to deal with it on their own. Research shows that for over 70 percent the only way for the bullying to stop is to quit. When this happens the bully has clearly won and will very likely find a new target.

People react to bullying in different ways. Some just let it happen, others get angry and retaliate, some become bullies and take out their anger on others (often their families), and others revert to extreme measures such as seriously injuring or killing the people that they feel are responsible for their being bullied and for others, the only way out for them is to commit (or attempt) suicide.

It is my belief that people who are being bullied can do something about it in a positive and safe way, which for them will have a positive outcome.

There is no set formula or step by step process. What I offer is a number of points which should be used as a guide. Also, the approach taken should vary based on the organizational culture, e.g. in a "Stable" culture, I encourage people to follow the process prescribed by the organization, because there the officials, usually Human Resources, can be trusted to act in the best interest of the person being bullied, conversely in a "Dictatorial" culture, I recommend that people deal with their situation outside the process prescribed by the organization, because there the officials, again usually Human Resources, should be viewed with scepticism, as they either have zero influence to stop the bullying, or they are part of the problem. In what I describe as a "Disjointed" culture, I advise caution on whether to follow the process prescribed by the organization, and suggest only going to an internal official that they have absolute trust in.

Much can be learned from the experiences of others. Bullying is not one off situations. Bullying in an organization or by an individual usually follows a pattern. People in an organization are usually aware of others who have been bullied in the past. Reaching out to these people and having them relate their experiences will provide valuable insight on what to do, and what to avoid, and who to trust.

To sum up my advice to people who are bullied, it is:

Anyone can be targeted, the key is to not succumb to it; and not let the situation control you. Be proactive instead of reactive—not everyone succumbs to the bullying.

If you are being bullied, I offer the following on what to do (and not do.)

1. *Don't deal with it alone*

> "Trouble is part of your life, and if you don't share it, you don't give the person who loves you a chance to love you enough."
>
> —Dinah Shore

Talk to someone who is close to you about it. This is not something you should be ashamed of. You are not the first and only person dealing with this. It is not your fault. People you are close to want to help you and can help you through this. You need someone to help you think through the steps we offer, challenge you and help you develop a strategy.

Don't hide the situation from your family, they need to know, as they can also be indirectly victims. Also, they will know something is wrong and will observe things about you that you may not be aware of, mood swings, disengagement, irritability etc., and if they are aware of what you are going through they can not only help you through it, they can help you build your sense of self which we believe is a prerequisite for taking an assertive position.

2. *Build your "Sense of Self"*

"No one can make you feel inferior without your consent."

—Eleanor Roosevelt

Accept the fact that the bully wants to break you. Don't succumb to it! If you are being bullied at work it takes over your life, it becomes your life, and it will lower your sense of self.

Understand who you are and what you offer, at home, in your community and at work. Many people withdraw from who they are when they are bullied. Do the opposite, become a better spouse, parent, son, daughter, friend, coach, mentor, volunteer, expert and producer. By feeling good about whom you are, what you do and what you offer will help you avoid the bullying from taking over your life. Exercise and the right diet are helpful in building on your sense of self when you go through this trauma.

Having this strong sense of self will also put you in a better frame of mind to deal with the bullying.

3. *Don't become a "Bullied Bully"*

A bullied bully is both a target and a bully. In what I call a Dictatorial culture the CEO is usually a CBO who bullies his direct reports, who in turn bully the front line managers, who in turn bully the front line employees. Bullied and abused by their superiors he bullies others to get some relief from his own feelings of powerlessness and self loathing. Least popular of all bullies, he strikes out viciously at those who do not respond to him, those who hurt him and those who are weaker targets.

Dictatorial and Disjointed cultures are usually full of bullied bullies. Often in these cultures people feel it is the only way to survive. They feel forced to behave in a manner that is inconsistent with their values and beliefs. Regardless of the culture in your organization, you cannot only survive you can excel by staying true to your values and beliefs and treating people with respect and dignity. By doing this you will garner the respect, loyalty and support of your peers and subordinates. Also, by doing this you will be a role model for others who are being bullied. From my perspective, there is no better way to build on your sense of self than to be above it all and not allow yourself to act and behave inconsistent with your value system.

Reacting this way to being bullied it is the most respectful form of revolt, and one that even the most powerful of bullies will have difficulty discrediting. As Mark Twain wrote, "Fewer things are harder to put up with than the annoyance of a good example."

4. *Validate the bullying*

"The man who is swimming against the stream knows the strength of it."

—Woodrow Wilson

Organizations have the right to discipline, demote and fire. As outlined earlier there are many ways and means of bullying. You may be discriminated against, but that does not necessarily constitute bullying, you may be teased, but that does not necessarily mean you are being bullied, you may be confronted, someone may flirt with you, you may be subject to an incident of impulsive aggression, again these acts do not necessarily constitute bullying. By understanding what bullying is and what it is not, and making distinctions (see "making Distinctions") will help validate whether or not bullying is occurring.

By validating in your own mind that bullying is occurring will put you on the offense rather than the defense when you decide to confront the situation. Bullies when confronted usually will say things like: "You are taking it the wrong way," "I don't mean to harm," "I'm passionate about the company and sometimes get carried away because of my passion," and "That's my style and I am only doing what is expected of me to improve performance." You must be ready for these pat answers by saying things like, "I understand, but these actions and behaviors constitute bullying."

Bullying is usually not one act. Bullies can be very subtle and manipulative and utilize a combination of a number of forms and ways of bullying. It is therefore important to tie seemingly unrelated, comments, events and situations to fully outline and put into context what is happening to you.

5. *Understand what is motivating the bullying*

As indicated earlier the primary reasons employees are targeted, they are;

- Retaliation
- Bigotry
- Exploitation
- Abuse of power

- Eliminate a threat

Knowing why you are being targeted will help you challenge the situation. Again, being able to assert or indicate that you strongly believe that you are being targeted will put you on the offense rather than on the defence. You are not likely the first or only target and as such whoever is dealing with the situation will not be able to ignore your assertion or belief. This combined with the actions and behaviors of the bully, gives you credibility, particularly if the person dealing with it relates it to other like situations he or she is aware of.

6. *Keep a detailed diary of what you are going through*

By documenting every comment, situation and event you will be better able to not only fully analyze what you are going through, you will be better able to state your position. Bullies discredit their targets. By having the facts, properly framed and marshalled, you will be able to turn the situation around by discrediting the bully. For obvious reasons bullies do not keep a running record of their actions and behaviors.

Bullies need to know that they will be held accountable for "creating unfavorable impressions," that are not true.

Record conversations you have with the bully. Small recorders that look like a pen are available at most electronic stores (some with video cameras are also available). Proof of these conversations proving abusive or threatening language will add credibility to your position. The bully may claim that recording the conversation is illegal, you counter that the bullies behavior is the illegal action here. It is not illegal as long as one of the parties are aware, you are one of the parties.

7. *Don't fall into The Bully's Trap*

> "I learned long ago never to wrestle with a pig. You get dirty, and besides the pig likes it."
>
> —Cyrus Ching

As we indicated earlier, bullies try to discredit their targets. The usual criticisms they lodge include, deteriorating performance, poor attitude, insubordination and ironically enough poor people skills. While bullies don't document their actions and behaviors, rest assured that they will be documenting yours to build up a case against you. The advice is, don't fall into this trap.

Although we know it will not be easy, but, rather than allow being bullied affect your performance or attitude, focus on excelling, keep your anger in check, and don't get sucked into a confrontation with the bully.

8. *Don't get set-up*

There are different ways and means of bullying. Bullies use tactics such as excluding you from essential meetings, giving you the wrong time for meetings to start, having you prepare for a topic different than what will be addressed, setting unreasonable expectations and measuring your performance based on subjectivity and ambiguity. By having clarity around meetings, timing of meetings, agenda's, expectations, and what you are measured on will help you avoid getting set up

Be assertive, get written confirmation on anything that the bully could set you up on. If you are not invited to a meeting that you should be at, go to the meeting anyway. If you are not receiving correspondence or reports that you should be getting, figure out a way to get them. The message here is to be sensitive to everything that is going on and be one or two steps ahead of the bully.

9. *Call the Bully on it*

Timing is key here, at the earliest opportunity you should make this request. Ideally the first step is to simply indicate to the bully that you do not appreciate being bullied and ask that it be stopped. Do it in a respectful manner, don't get into a debate, just indicate that you know that you are being bullied and want it to stop. Bullies are not used to being called on their actions and behaviors, this direct request could possibly disarm him and have the bullying stop.

If the bully wants to debate the issue indicate that you are happy to do so, but you want a witness present. The witness should either be the bullies' immediate superior or a human resource representative. By having a detailed diary of the comments, events and situations helps you control of the situation.

At this session, do not accept rationalizations like, this is a style issue or a personality clash. Also, don't accept a conflict resolution approach, because this suggests that you are in a fight with the bully. Bullying is not a fight, it takes two or more to fight, bullying is one sided and you are on the receiving end. The purpose of the session is to register your expectation that the bullying stop. You should also put them on notice that if the bullying does not stop and/or you are retaliated against because you made this request you will take further steps.

If the bullying persists and/or you are being retaliated against register your complaint with someone in the organization who you have absolute trust in. In a Stable culture it should be the head of human resources, in a Dictatorial or Disjointed culture it could be the person in charge of legal or internal audit.

"A fox should not be the jury at a goose's trial."
—Thomas Fuller

If the organization initiates an investigation, make sure you sign off on how the investigation will be conducted and who will be interviewed. You should be assured that the investigation does not become a "kangaroo court," where you become the person where a disproportionate focus of the investigation is on you. In the section "Human Resources part of the problem part of the solution". We provide advice to human resource people on conducting investigations involving bullying.

10. *Get professional help*

If you believe that you are being set up to be fired or you have lost control of the situation, seek advice from an employment lawyer, or if you are represented by a union, your union representative. Armed with your detailed diary you will get professional advice on what your legal options are. Courts are becoming less tolerant of employers who condone and/or encourage bullying. Remember, if you have your facts properly framed and marshalled, you are in a better position to take control, or regain control of the situation, this time by involving external help and potentially seeking legal recourse.

Research shows that most of the people who are bullied suffer from "Post Traumatic Stress Disorder." The stress of being bullied can and does affect your physical and mental health. In some cases it can lead people to take drastic action, the most extreme being murder and suicide. Like our first point, "Don't deal with it alone," if you are having symptoms don't deal with it alone, seek medical help. Remember, there should be no shame in what you are going through, and it is not your fault. If you don't properly deal with the symptoms, you will allow the situation to control you and it could lead to an extremely bad outcome.

11. Help start the revolution for change

"A good indignation brings out all one's powers."

—Ralph Waldo Emerson

You as a bullied employee are also very likely a bystander, particularly if you work in a Dictatorial or Disjointed culture. Having been bullied and being in control of the situation and stopping it you are in a powerful position to change it. While I have cautioned against anger, I encourage indignation, and this indignation against what you went through should also carry forward to what others in the organization are going through.

"Let us not look back in anger or forward in fear, but around in awareness."

—James Thurber

Defining the Unjust— Advice to the Bystander

> First they came for the communists, and I didn't speak out because I wasn't a communist. Then they came for the trade unionists, and I didn't speak out because I wasn't a trade unionist. Then they came for the Jews, and I didn't speak out because I wasn't a Jew. Then they came for me and there was no one left to speak for me.
>
> —Marten Niemollers

In the course of your working career, you will be exposed to bullying and be a bystander. When this happens, you have to make choices, do nothing, actively or passively support the bully, or become a witness and or defender and or a resistor.

Choosing to be a witness or a defender or resister is not free of risk; this requires courage. Choosing not to be a witness, defender, or activist is also not free of risk when you consider:

- Could I have helped avoid a physical or mental breakdown?
- Could I have helped avoid ruining a career?
- Could I have helped avoid a family breakdown?
- Could I have helped avoid the organizations downfall?
- Could I have helped avoid a suicide (or attempted suicide?)
- Could I have helped avoid a murder?

All of these are real risks that I believe outweigh the risk of being a witness, defender and activist.

In making this choice, knowing there is risk, the way you handle it will help minimize the risk to you and the target. Do not be impulsive or reckless, what you do must be fact based, handled with great sensitivity, tact and respect.

We offer the following advice on how you can help or try to help the target:

1. *Become a witness*

    When you either observe bullying or suspect that someone is being bullied, start taking notes of what you hear and see.

    Even though the bullying may be subtle, there are lots of indicators.

    The main indicators are how the target reacts to the bullying. (Change in personality, withdrawn, disengaged, lashing out, slippage in performance, higher absenteeism, signs of substance abuse, negative comments about the organization and management, and other behaviors or comments that are uncharacteristic.)

    The other indicators include comments made by other bystanders, the water cooler chit chat, gossip, comments made by the bully (remember the bully is intent on discrediting the target), and the target being excluded from situations and correspondence that he/she would normally be part of. As this is likely not the bullies first target, recalling previous situations you are aware of and comparing them to this situation can reveal other indicators.

    As in our advice to the bullied by having facts properly framed and marshalled, if you register that bullying is occurring, your evidence will carry a lot of weight. Remember, bullies are unlikely to keep a running record of their actions and behaviors.

2. *Validate the bullying*

We have outlined what constitutes bullying and what doesn't. Organizations have the right to discipline, demote and fire. You may have a legitimate reason to challenge these decisions, but they do not necessarily constitute bullying. By understanding what bullying is and what it is not, and making distinctions like teasing vs. taunting will help validate whether or not bullying is occurring.

Bullying is usually not one act. In the chapter "The Bully," we outlined the many forms, ways and means of bullying. Bullies can be very subtle and manipulative and utilize a combination of a number of these forms, ways and means. It is therefore important to tie seemingly unrelated, comments, events and situations to fully outline and put into context what is happening to the target.

3. *Become outraged*

Most instances of the physical aggression have a common thread, which is, that bullying goes on without substantial objections, indignation, adequate intervention or outrage. We are devastated by that final act of violence but rarely outraged by the events that led to the final act.

4. *Reach out to the target*

In our advice to the bullied, the first piece of advice we give is, "Don't deal with it alone."

The target is in a lonely place and does not believe that there is anyone who can or will help.

Go to the target and say, "I think I know you are being bullied, is there anything I can do to help?" This approach will let the target know they are not alone, and it will also confirm what he suspects. If the target is too ashamed to acknowledge that he is being bullied, relay to her your observations and if there is a pattern of bullying, indicate that they are not the first target.

5. *Help the target "Build Sense of Self"*

Building a strong sense of self is the prerequisite to be able to control the situation and not be controlled by it.

You are in a unique position to help him do this. Assuming you know the target you can highlight the positive attributes he has. You can also contrast the positives with what you observe as negative reactions to being bullied and help him make the assessment that his sense of self is being compromised by the bully.

6. *Help the target become assertive*

    The first step is point five, helping the target build sense of self. The next steps are helping him to follow points four through nine in "Advise to the Bullied"

    - "Validate whether you are being bullied."
    - "Understand what is motivating the bully.
    - "Keep a detailed diary of what you are going through."
    - "Don't fall into *The Bully's Trap*."
    - "Avoid getting set up."
    - "Make a formal request to have the bullying stop."

    All of these are things usually fall outside of peoples comfort zone and as such to help, coach, support and provide constructive criticism is extremely beneficial to the target.

7. *Avoid having the target do harm to himself or others*

    If you feel that the target needs professional help, encourage him to seek it. Here you may have to go to the target's family or other friends for a proper intervention.

    If you feel that the target has the potential of harming himself or others you must report the situation to someone in authority. In section, "Human Resources—part of the problem or part of the solution," I outline indicators to watch out for. These red flags are always evident and most extreme examples of violence could have been avoided if there were early intervention. Most leaders do not view verbal or psychological abuse as violence or make the connection that these types of predatory aggression give rise to the physical aggression (by both the bullied and the bully.) Fill the void of leadership here and make the connection.

When you report this, you are not being disloyal to the target, you are not a snitch; you are protecting the target and others who potentially could get seriously injured or killed.

8. *Request that the bully stop the bullying*

If the target is not able to handle the situation and you have a solid enough relationship with the bully, indicate that you know what is going on and that it would be in his best interest to stop the bullying. It is advisable to point out that you are on to him through your own observations and that the target did not complain to you.

Alternatively if your relationship with the bully is not solid, but is solid with the bully's immediate superior, make the request that he intervene.

9. *Formally register and report*

If point number eight is not feasible or has backfired on you, you should report the situation to someone in authority that you have absolute trust in. If there is no one that you have confidence in to properly intervene and keep it confidential, protecting both you and the target, you should consider two options:

- Submit the report to either the organizations legal counsel or external auditor (with the understanding that you will not be revealed as the source of the report and the target will not be retaliated against.)

or

- Send the report anonymously to the organizations lawyer. If this is the route you take the report should identify the bully and outline as much as you can without identifying you as the source or the target. Also, you should outline your expectation that the matter will be properly investigated and that the bullying stop. If the bullying continues and/or you and the target are subject to retaliation, file a report with the Chair of the board of directors pointing out that the report was sent to the company's lawyer and what happened as a result.

10. *Hold the organization and its leaders accountable*

When you report you must be very clear on your motivation, which is to have the bullying stop. Without having it sound like blackmail, indicate that if the situation is not properly investigated and the bullying does not stop, or you and the target experience retaliation, that you will take the matter further. (You don't have to say what further is.)

11. *Help start the revolution for change*

As the bystander you are in a powerful position to change it while we caution against anger, I encourage indignation against what the targets and others in the organization are going through.

12. *Build on your "Sense of Self"*

Recognize that your choice to become a witness, defender, and activist has significantly strengthened your "Sense of Self"—*Congratulations*!

Redemption—Advice to the Bully

> You've got to be brave and you've got to be bold. Brave enough to take your chance on your own discrimination—what's right and what's wrong, what's good and what's bad.
>
> —Robert Frost

My advice to those who bully is simply stop bullying, and change or be changed.

Our research shows that the majority of bullies are what I refer to as "bullied bullies." These people usually work in cultures that condone, encourage and expect their managers to motivate by fear and intimidation and have CEOs who are also CBOs (Chief Bullying Officers). Many of these people behave outside of their value system, and all too many love to exert their power though bullying. Sadly for many, bullying is the only way they know how to get things done.

Most of the bullies I have dealt with were unhappy people who did not even like themselves are therefore had no problem being mean to others.

One of the purposes of the book is to "help bullies change". In the introduction I outline the eleven things I believe that needs to happen for bullying to stop.

Regarding the bully, I believe:

- That an employee index be a major component on how managers are measured.
- Bullies need to be held accountable for their behaviors and actions.

- Where workplace bullying is a factor in a suicide, the organization and the bully should face criminal charges.
- Where workplace bullying causes major harm the organization and the bully should face criminal and/or civil charges.

Another purpose of this book is to raise the level of awareness, and by raising the level of awareness, help empower both the target and the bystanders force the bullying to stop and hold the organization and the bully accountable for their behaviors and actions.

While I raise the level of awareness on the risks and the costs of bullying to the individual, the family unit, the organization, and the community, I found that what really resonates with the bully is the risk they could face.

For me, if the motive for a bully to stop bullying is risk avoidance, that is sufficient, not ideal, but sufficient.

I offer the following advice to the bully:

1. *If you are the CBO (Chief Bullying Officer), really study this book.*

    Unless you change or are changed, your organization will operate in a culture of fear, you will not hear what you need to hear, your organization will not reach its full potential, the best and the brightest will not stay or join and you place your organization at risk. While we believe that bullies in your organization can stop being bullies, if you are a bully it will obviously be difficult for them to do so.

2. *Understand what constitutes bullying and what does not.*

    If you are a manager, you are expected to manage and part of managing is to correct deficiencies and attitudes. As there are ways and means of bullying, there are ways and means of positively motivating, managing, leading and correcting deficiencies and attitudes. While this is beyond the scope of this book, there is ample work done on this and whether through your employer or on your own you should educate yourself on how to get things done without having to bully.

3. *Know your rights, and exercise them.*

Because you are bullied is no excuse to be a bully. If bullying is the only way to either survive or get ahead in your organization you should seriously think about making a change. Ultimately you will get caught and have to face the consequences of your behaviors and actions, which could include facing criminal and/or civil charges.

4. *Understand the devastating impact that bullying can have on the individual, the family unit, the organization and the community.*

I believe that everyone can and should be able to relate to this as at some point in everyone's life they have been a target and/or a bystander, and/or have had someone close to them been a target. By personalizing the impact of bullying, you are better able to conclude that you have to change.

5. *Don't deal with it alone; seek the advice and help of others.*

If you can identify someone in your organization who is a role model who survives and thrives without being a bully, go to that person and ask his or her advice. Other options are to seek the help of a career coach or psychologist. Many organizations will sponsor this, if they don't, it is a personal investment that will yield a return.

6. *Reach out to those you have bullied and apologize.*

Indicate to them that you genuinely want to change and that you want their help by calling you on situations when you cross the line.

7. *Become a role model of someone who survives and thrives without being a bully.*

I encourage bullies to seek redemption; the prerequisite to this is caring. If you don't care for your fellow human being you will have great difficulty in changing your behaviours. Nelson Mandela, in his *Long Walk to Freedom* put it so well when he wrote, "No one is born hating another person because of the colour of his skin, or his background, or his religion. People must learn to hate, and if they can learn to hate, they can be taught to love, for love comes more naturally to the human heart than it's opposite."

Is Someone Close to You Being Bullied—Advice to Families And Friends

"The fundamental law of human beings is interdependence. A person is a person through other persons."

—Archbishop Desmond Tutu

In my advice to the bullied, the first recommendation is: Don't deal with it alone. It should not be assumed that if a family member or close friend who is bullied will follow this advice. What they are going through is destroying their sense of self and it is very difficult for them to admit to this. You must reflect on the reasons they may keep the information from you.

The Clues

As a family member or close friend you will know, something is wrong based on changes you see. : You are in the best position to help the bullied through what they are going through. If they know that they can come to you with the good, the bad and the ugly, and that you will actively listen and offer support, guidance, and wisdom, there is a chance they might tell you that they are being bullied. Even though they may not come right out and tell you, by engaging them in a dialogue about work you will find clues that something is wrong. When you see these warning signs or clues that your family member or friend is being bullied, listen beyond the words and look beyond the actions: Someone who is being bullied will:

- Be doing things out of character.
- Be sad, sullen, angry, or scared after receiving a phone call or an e mail.
- Stop talking about work. Show an abrupt lack of interest in work.
- Be always on edge.
- Withdraw from family and social activities, wanting to be left alone.
- Lash out at family members and close friends.
- Use derogatory or demeaning language when talking about the organization, boss or peers.
- Start taking more time off.
- Engage in substance abuse.
- Has stomach aches, headaches, panic attacks, be unable to sleep, or sleep too much and is still exhausted.
- Stop exercising and not taking proper care of self.

If you see these warning signs or clues an intervention may be required. The best approach is to ask them directly if they are having a problem at work. Indicate that bullying in the workplace is common and if they are experiencing this that you want to help them through it.

A Few Do's and Don'ts

In having the dialogue, the key is to have the bullied think through what they are going through, that means you need to actively listen to them. You need to make them comfortable in knowing that your help will be instructive and constructive—not make the situation worse. They need to count on the following messages from you:

1. "I hear you; I am here for you; I believe you; you are not alone in this."

   No matter what the bullied has to say or how he is saying it, a good line for you is "Tell me about it", then be quiet and listen. Asking him to talk about the bullying without asking a lot of questions up front to frame his answers will give you insight into his perceptions, concerns and anxieties. You may be able to get at the reasons why the bullying might have cut into the core of his sense of dignity and self worth. (Is he beating himself up for being bullied? Is he ashamed of the way he is responding or not responding to the bully? Is he being humiliated by his peers who are supporting the bully and abandoned or shunned him?)

   After he has talked about his own hurt and pain, you can begin to gather the facts. To jump immediately to the facts is to miss the most important impact of the bullying—what it has done to his sense of well being.

2. "It is not your fault."

   The blame belongs to the bully. No one deserves to be bullied. There may be things that the bullied has done that aggravate or annoy the bully, but nothing justifies the contemptuous behavior of the bully. This is no time for "If you didn't... If you weren't so..." Remember, the bully has already demeaned him and he needs your help to counteract the ugly injunctions.

3. "You are a good person"

   Help the bullied build a stronger sense of self. This is one of the, if not the most important things you can do. Remind him of past successes, how good a father and spouse he is, what he does well, how respected he is. Encourage him to focus on activities outside of work—hobbies, friends, volunteer activities. With a stronger sense of self, he is better equipped mentally to cope and deal with the situation by being more assertive that he is with a low sense of self.

4. "How can I help"

    Other points you can make are: "You are not helpless or hopeless and you are not alone. Together we can come up with an effective plan." You can help figure out ways for her to assertively stand up to the bully, steer clear of dangerous situations, take her power back, and more fully develop the gifts and skills she has. She will need your help to explore options, analyze choices, and eliminate those that would make the situation worse or put her in more danger or provoke more bullying.

There are five things you don't want to do:

1. Don't minimize, rationalize, or explain away the bully's behaviour

    Bullying hurts a lot. No, the bully wasn't just teasing or flirting or having a conflict; and yes the bully intended harm. By minimizing, rationalizing, or trying to explain away the behavior of the bully, you are inadvertently telling the bullied that she is in this all alone. It won't take her long to figure it's best to suffer in silence.

2. Don't tell the bullied to quit

    The majority of people who are bullied quit because they believe that it is the only way to stop the bullying. Leaving an organization is an option, but it should not be the first one.

3. Don't tell the bullied to stay out of the bully's way

   This is not a realistic approach, the bully will not allow it. By trying to avoid contact with the bully all you do is give them more ammunition to discredit the bullied.

4. Don't tell the bullied to immediately confront the bully

   Confronting the bully needs to be well thought through. Every possible reaction needs to be played out. If the bully has her in his trap, she needs to be prepared to discredit him, which requires a comprehensive statement of the facts, from when the bullying started.

5. Don't try to handle the situation

   Remember that the bullied sense of self is likely very low because of the experience he is going through. By taking control of the situation will make him feel more out of control. You should be there to help him through it, by having him become assertive, and to be assertive he has to have a strong sense of self.

Seeking Professional Help

If you believe that the bullied family member or friend could be of danger to himself or others insist that he seek professional help. If he refuses this, you need to advise his employer so that they are aware that there is a risk and they can force an intervention. Similarly if you see a significant deterioration in his physical health, professional help should be sought.

The Unthinkable

The sad reality is that bullying is a factor in suicides or attempted suicides. If bullying is a factor in a family member's suicide or attempted suicide, you should hold the bully and the organization accountable by seeking a criminal charge and/or filing a civil suit against them.

The other sad reality is that bullying is a factor when an employee causes serious harm including killing others. If bullying is a factor, if a family member or close friend goes to this extreme, the bully and the organization has to bear some of the responsibly, because of the bullying and not preventing the outcome by being aware of the warning signs. You must be the advocate of this.

A Happy Ending—John's Story

John is the CEO of a large manufacturing company established by his Grandparents in 1927. The company now produces private label products for many of the grocery chains across North America. The company is privately held and the family own the controlling shares. There are six manufacturing facilities, all of which operate as non union, which is a source of great pride to John and the other family members. Despite having to make some labor adjustments the company has enjoyed good relations with their employees.

In 2002 John was able to attract Ryan to run the Ajax Plant, their second largest facility. Ryan came with the right pedigree, having spent the bulk of his career in operations with a global packaged goods company. During the extensive interview process Ryan said all of the right things and impressed John and the others on the selection committee. They thought he was the right fit with values that were consistent with those of the company's. Ryan was the first outsider in the company's history to be brought in at this level.

Although there were some operating parameters and quality standards John allowed each facility to operate with a lot of autonomy as he believed that entrepreneurship was a key to getting superior results.

By all metrics, Ryan was doing a great job. Revenues, profitability, quality and service levels all exceeded plan on a consistent basis.

A number of years earlier John introduced a balanced scorecard for the business and all departments and facilities were measured on the financials, an employee index and a customer index. Every year an employee attitude survey was conducted. Ryan's facility always scored high, although the participation rate was on average around 70 percent, not as high as the other departments and facilities.

In 2006 the company received notice that the Ajax Plant was the target of a union organizing drive.

Given the results of the employee engagement survey conducted only six months ago this action came as a complete surprise. John's initial reaction was to trust Mary, the company[1]s Vice President of Human Resources and Ryan, and their advice to do everything possible to keep the union out. John, after all, had the perception that a union would make the plant non competitive, with rising salaries, limited productivity and restrictive work practices. Mary was responsible for developing the plan to keep the union out. She immediately retained a law firm who had a reputation for union avoidance and union busting, a firm she worked with at her previous employer. Ryan was responsible for all of the activities that were not handled by the labor lawyer.

The plan that Mary developed involved all of the legal tactics that are usually employed and included a number of tactics that definitely crossed the line. People who were thought to be ring leaders of the drive had their phones monitored, some were even put under surveillance. Through a third party a senior person in the union was offered a bribe. Managers and supervisors were coached on how to give subtle messages on what the consequences would be if employees signed cards and when the time came to vote, if they voted to certify.

In an interview with the press John indicated that the union would make the facility uncompetitive and they would have to relocate. A capacity study was done and John and others made it know that there was ample capacity in their other facilities to move all of the production. A number of employees were fired with trumped up allegations of wrong doing that John was not aware of. All new hires were plants to keep Ryan informed of who was doing what. Each time they came to Ryan with info they received under the table cash. Employees were pitted against employees, and emotions ran high. The legal and surveillance bills went into the hundreds of thousands of dollars.

Throughout all of this Ryan was in his element, every time he spoke to John he said, "We are going to win, those bastards don't know who they are dealing with."

John kept his Board of Directors apprised of the situation. At a Board meeting, three months into it one of the three Independent Board members asked John, "Why do the employees there feel they need a third party to represent them?" John indicated that he was perplexed by it, employees there and at the other facilities had a pay rate and benefits that were slightly ahead of competitors who were unionized and "we treat them well and with respect, this is something that we measure every year in our employee attitude survey." The Board member then asked John whether there were any indicators of discontent that he observed during his visit to the facility prior to the union drive. John appeared a bit flushed and answered, "No," which was technically an honest answer but he failed to mention that he had not visited the facility in two years, and when he did, he did not go beyond the office.

The questions bothered John; he realized that he was not close enough to the operations. All he looked at was the results but not how the results were achieved. He needed more points of reference. John recalled that there were a couple of managers he knew who recently resigned from the Ajax plant and called them and asked them to meet him.

They met the next day and what the former managers told John confirmed John's worst fears. From the time Ryan took over the facility it was run like a dictatorship. Ryan bullied the managers, who in turn bullied the supervisors who bullied the rank and file. Performance was achieved through harassment, threats and fear. Specific examples were given which were appalling to John. "Why didn't you come to me with this?" John asked. The response that came back was, "Ryan would ruin us if he ever found out, and everyone who works there shares this concern." John cited the employee engagement survey results to which the former managers said employees don't trust it and if the results came back negative Ryan would go on a witch hunt and punish those who did not play along.

The former managers recommended to John that he review things like the turnover rate, absentee records, number of people who have been on stress leave, lack of comments made on the engagement surveys, and the fact that very few employees including them were afraid to do an exit interview. They also suggested that John check out the relationship that Ryan had with the companies that Ryan had given the contracts to, when the company decided to third party janitorial and maintenance activities "you may find they are related to Ryan's wife" one of them said.

After this meeting John contacted Mary and asked her to investigate what the former managers had conveyed and he wanted to meet with her the next day to review. The next day Mary reported to John, turnover at the plant ran on average 12 percent for production and distribution employees for the last five years and a astounding 30 percent for managers and supervisors, the absentee rate was significantly higher at Ajax than at the other facilities, applications for stress leaves were high but in most cases challenged by the insurance provider at the request of the plant human resource manager. Mary also indicated that accidents were usually covered up and anyone with a lost time accident usually went on salary continuation to protect their experience ratings. On the relationship with the third party providers Mary said she had heard rumours to this effect but she did not follow up because she was afraid of Ryan as well. "What else do you know?" John asked. Mary admitted that she was aware that there were problems but had no idea that it was as bad as it was. "Why didn't you come to me? John asked. Mary responded by saying that the engagement surveys did not validate what she was hearing. "Well obviously the surveys are not worth the paper their written on" John reacted in exasperation.

All of this was a rude awakening for John, he felt frustrated with himself, betrayed, and seriously questioned whether he was now equipped to fix everything that was wrong. He also felt if he was so out of the loop regarding the Ajax plant, how different would he find the situation at the other facilities.

A meeting of the Board was called and John laid out the whole situation to them with a plan. First however, he volunteered to resign if the Board lost confidence in him and if they did he would completely understand. The Board gave John the vote of confidence with the qualifier that he needed to take a more hands on approach in running the company. The Board also unanimously agreed with the plan John had developed.

The first step was to deal with Ryan. John confronted him with what he heard. While Ryan vehemently defended what he referred to as his "aggressive management style," citing the consistent results he had delivered, proving that it works, he could not deny that the outside contractors were owned by this brother in-law's and he did not declare a conflict of interest. John asked for and received his resignation.

John then met with the President of the union and indicated that the company had put an immediate stop to the actions to avoid the Ajax plant from becoming certified and would agree to have an employees vote on whether they wanted representation. Further he indicated that he wanted to meet with the employees as a group to let them know that if they elected to be represented, the company would respect their decision and he would retract the comments and threats to close the plant and declare that in his view the plant was a solid performer and could continue to be if it were unionized.

A vote was conducted two weeks later and the employees voted to become represented by a high margin. A first agreement was negotiated in record time and as the wages and benefits were already a bit ahead of the unionized competitors the company and the union agreed to an incentive program that rewarded productivity, quality and service level targets.

Concurrently a consulting firm was hired to do a thorough cultural assessment of the organization and report back with recommendations within a months' time. The primary objective the company wanted to achieve was to gain the trust of the employees at all of their facilities. John received the report a month later and followed all of the recommendations made in the report with one exception which was to continue to do an engagement survey. His rational for this was they had done this over the years and it failed to reveal how employees felt, because, if employees do not trust leadership they will not trust any mechanism to gauge attitudes. "From now on we are going to hear directly from our employees because they will not be afraid to express their feelings, concerns or ideas," he declared.

As a result of going through all this proved very beneficial to the company, not only did it survive the economic downturn, it prospered. The Ajax plant became the number one performer and all of the other facilities exceeded their targets. The company grew during this period adding staff. Turnover, absenteeism, accidents all decreased dramatically. Employees at all of the facilities enjoyed compensation that well exceeded the market because the incentive program first introduced as a result of the first agreement at Ajax was also implemented at the other facilities. The company enjoyed a great relationship with the union and as John indicated to the union President, they were "not at all concerned about our other plants being unionized because we are going to make sure they never feel that they need a third party to represent them" the other five facilities and one they added since, are non union.

Attitude or engagement surveys are not conducted, instead quarterly town hall type meetings are held with all shifts in all facilities. John attends each and every one and communicates results and plans going forward, and opens the meetings for questions and comments. Today there based on the honest exchanges that take place there does not appear to be a lack of trust.

Investor's Business Daily spent years analyzing leaders and successful people in all walks of life and they identified ten traits. John's story is an excellent example of their tenth point, which is: "Be Honest and Dependable; Take Responsibility." They point out the key is how well you work with your organization to regain trust. The tips they give are: "bite the bullet, take control, make it right, avoid pitfalls, look through another lens, encourage honesty, solve problems faster, set the standard and move on." John using his value system and his intuition as a leader followed all of these tips, and some.

Employee Activists—Forcing a Cultural Transformation

The closing case study, "A Happy Ending—John's Story," outlines how a positive cultural change was forced because of a union organizing drive. This is a rare exception as organizing drives are vigorously fought by employers and usually makes an already bad situation worse.

As I argue in this book, for bullying to stop it requires an organizational transformation. Hopefully leaders will see the benefit and logic of my argument and initiate the change. Given the entrenched attitudes that exist, I would not bank on it.

My introduction to the book begins with a quote from Mahatma Gandhi:

"It is possible for a single individual to defy the whole might of an unjust empire to save his honour, his religion, his soul, and lay the foundation for that empire's fall or it's regeneration." These powerful words are a clarion call to all who work in toxic cultures.

Just as shareholder activists can force a shift in strategy, the composition of the board, or a change in leadership, employees as key stakeholders can force a change in culture.

Bullying in the workplace puts the organization at risk and the impacts are enormous.

The International Federation of Accountants at the United Nations Conference on Trade Development in 2010 concluded that "positioning risk management as a key board responsibility" and that "Governance is more than having the right structures, regulation and principles in place—it is about ensuring that the right behaviours and processes are in place."

Employees are in the best position to ensure the board is made aware of the risk.

A first step is engaging others in the organization that share your concern, and whom you absolutely trust. Ideally this group is representative of a cross section of the organization.

The following is an example, which illustrates how your concerns could be framed.

Statement of Claim

1. We are a group of (X) employees, representing a cross section of the company who are concerned that the toxic culture that exists poses a risk to the organization and all of its stakeholders.

2. We are bringing our concerns forward so that you can ensure that the right behaviours and processes are in place.

3. Our intention and expectation is that the bullying stop.

4. The following outlines recent examples of bullying: (list the examples and provide documentation, e.g. emails, comments on a blog or other social media, video or sound recordings)

5. We recommend the following:

    - an investigation of the examples we have provided
    - a cultural audit (here you can provide a copy of "Conducting a Workplace Assessment—Determining a At Risk Position" Appendix 2)
    - appropriate action to ensure the bullying stops

6. We have brought this matter to your attention in good faith and assume no attempt will be made to identify the

source of this action, i.e. a 'Witch Hunt' and no retaliatory action will be taken.

7. If you in conducting the investigation have questions of us, they can be forwarded to (recommend obtaining a safe P.O. Box that is difficult to trace).

The statement of claim should be sent by registered post to either the head of human resources or the organization's lawyer with a copy to the Chair of Audit of the board.

If after sixty days there is no change in behaviours, a follow up should be sent indicating that the situation has not changed (or has gotten worse). In this you should request a response to the P.O. Box outlining the organization's position on the matter.

If after thirty days no response is provided, you should send a letter indicating that you will be exposing the situation to major shareholders or the media.

If you or others suspect a "witch hunt" or retaliation, seek immediate legal advice.

*

And in conclusion

The following is the commencement address given to graduates of a College of Applied Arts and Technology in Ontario, Canada, in June of 2011.

> By many standards I have lived a charmed and successful life. Like everyone, there have been setbacks, challenges and personal tragedies, all of which helped define who I am and what I stand for.
> Six years ago, being diagnosed with leukemia and given a life sentence was one of those challenges. Were it not for a miracle drug which turned what was a fatal condition to a chronic one, I would be dead today. This experience forced me to reflect on the reason for being, and discovering that notwithstanding the successes enjoyed, there was a void

which was, really having made a difference. What was missing was a lack of purpose.

Today my life is full of purpose, reflected in part through my philanthropy, but to a greater extent it is putting a stop to what I believe to be an epidemic—bullying in the workplace.

There is no need for me to explain to you what bullying is and the devastating impact it has other than to say bullying in schools shares many of the characteristics with bullying in the work place.

As there are similarities there are differences, the most significant being the ways and means are more subtle and there are fewer avenues for people to exit from the situation.

Bullies are masters of deflection, usually they discredit their targets to the point the target become the villain. They "kiss up and kick down." Because they are viewed as high performers they are treated like heroes who garner more credibility than the target.

The mighty have fallen because of organizational cultures that condone and encourage bullying.

In analyzing the demise of Enron, AIG, Lehmann Bothers, and the list goes on, they all had a common characteristic, which was their CEO's were also CBO's—Chief Bullying Officer's.

The global financial meltdown could have been avoided had people who were in the know, reported wrongdoings. They did not, largely for fear of being retaliated against. In most cases whistleblowers are viewed as traitors and subject to bullying as punishment for their treason.

Bullying has always occurred, however it shames me to say that my generation has systematically, largely because of greed, created dictatorial leadership, where fear has become a substitute for motivation and positive leadership.

We have allowed tyranny and domination to dictate the culture in which to work.

This is the sad legacy that my generation leaves to you.

Many have expressed, stopping this epidemic is "mission impossible."

For us it is not a question of "Can it be stopped?" It is an assertion: "It must be stopped." For it to be eliminated, everyone has a role to play.

Everyone graduating today will, at some point in your career, become a bully, and/or be bullied and/or be a bystander.

If history is any indicator only a small percent of you will become defenders of those who are bullied.

Where there has been genocide, which is the most extreme form of bullying, only a small percent of the population became witness and defenders of those who were targeted. Had the small percent been a mere ten percent, the course of history would have had a different outcome.

The revolutions in the Middle East, with the over through of tyranny is proof positive that the course of history can be changed, and serves as an inspiration to have the small percent become ten percent.

Over your careers you will be faced with choices. The most difficult ones for you will be whether or not to be a witness and defender of those who are targeted, becoming part of the ten percent.

This choice involves risk, and requires courage. The risks of being a witness and defender are obvious. However, in making the risk assessment, consider the risk of not being that witness and defender.

Consider never having to say,

- I could have prevented the ruin of my coworker's career.

Consider never having to say,

- I could have prevented the breakup of a family unit.

Consider never having to say,

- I could have helped avoid the demise of an organization.

Consider never having to say,
- I could have prevented a suicide or attempted suicide.

Consider never having to say,
- I could have prevented someone going postal and killing others.

    Mahatma Gandhi put it so well when he declared, "It is possible for a single individual to defy the whole might of an unjust empire to save his honour, his religion, his soul, and lay the foundation for that empire's fall or its regeneration."

    As this choice involves risk, it also yields rewards, the greatest of which is strengthening your sense of self, helping to make right what is wrong and making the lives of others free and safe from the ravages of tyranny.

    By becoming part of that ten percent, you can change the course of history.

Author's Note

Organizational transformation will be the focus of my next book. My hope is to tell the stories of where there have been successful transformations, the resulting impacts and how the change occurred. To help me on this, I encourage those who have experienced this kind of positive change to send me your story at andrew@bullyingattheworkplace.com

Appendices

I have included four Appendices:

1. Cyber-Bullying—High Tech Harassment by Glenn Pound
2. Conducting A Workplace Assessment—Determining 'At Risk' Position by Susan Shaw and Andrew Faas
3. Bullying and Performance Management by David Poirier and Andrew Faas
4. Whistleblower Protection: Creeping Towards A Solution by Richard Alderson

David, Richard, Susan, and I are Associates at Iceburg Navigation, a consulting firm that helps organizations transform their cultures. Glenn was commissioned to conduct research for the Author.

Cyber-Bullying—
High Tech Harassment

© Iceberg Navigation, 2011. Used with permission (commissioned and researched by Glenn Pound).

The incredible ubiquity of communication technologies in our lives has combined to spawn new forms of bullying and harassment, which can often prove far more damaging than traditional forms of bullying. The problem of cyber-bullying has grown to the extent that it is now often considered a major category of bullying. Just like face-to-face bullying, it is recognized as a very serious problem among adolescents, teens, and college students, but there has been less attention and research on cyber-bullying in the workplace. According to the United States National Crime Prevention Council, cyber-bullying occurs "when the Internet, cell phones or other devices are used to send or post text or images intended to hurt or embarrass another person."

Cyber-bullying is that technology allows bullies to act under a veil of anonymity, which often increases their numbers and the harm they spread. Emboldened, cyber-bullies hide behind screen names and multiply electronic addresses. They do not rely on physical power differences, but they still seek to control their victims by inflicting verbal, emotional, or psychological abuse. Interestingly, females are more than males to be cyber-bullies.

Technology also affords bullies 24/7 access to targets, and opens the opportunity for persistent, unending harassment from which victims are hard-pressed to escape. The instantaneous nature of online communications allows bullies to act on impulse and erases the reflection time between planning and execution. Online forums allow mobs to form quickly and almost effortlessly, drawing more people into the offensive activity. In sum, technology allows bullies to be more hurtful, more frequently, with more allies, before huge audiences.

The Toolkit

The target doesn't have to be onsite for the bully to act. It can happen at the dinner table. They can send nasty e-mails or text messages behind the victim's back. They can use camera phones to capture unflattering pictures that can be quickly distributed via web or e-mail. They can engage the victim in an Instant Messaging conversation, trick the person into revealing sensitive information, and then forward that information to others as a "joke." They can participate in chat rooms in which coworkers are taunted and belittled; they can set-up web sites whose sole purpose is to disgrace another; they can establish virtual polling places and rate coworkers in malicious ways. They can use e-mail to provoke the victim into a compromising, inappropriate, or angered response and then forward that to a boss, or others, out of context. They can use all of these forms to sabotage others, misinform, discredit, and set them up for failure; and they can often do so anonymously.

Employers and managers can also use all of these methods to bully their staff. One obvious application of these technologies would be that bosses can now apply pressure and ride their staff on a 24/7 basis. As technologies continue to evolve, cyber-bullies will doubtlessly adapt new ways to abuse their victims.

Bystanders

Again, like face-to-face bullying, bystanders are also affected by and involved in bullying, both actively and passively. Passive bystanders typically observe bullying but lack the self-confidence to intervene or assist. Bystanders typically choose not to intervene because they dread becoming the bully's next target or worry about making the situation worse, or simply do not know what to do. Active bystanders might support the bully, or actively participate in the bullying. Experts agree that when people persistently witness bullying, and nothing is done to stop it, they may begin to blame the victim for the problem as a way of rationalizing and coping with this behaviour. Many go further and begin to approve of or even participate in the bullying.

Anonymity can increase the odds of bystanders supporting bullies and participating in their bad acts. Studies of crowd behaviour show that members who perceive they are anonymous are more likely to shed their inhibitions and act in antisocial ways; they also are subject to increased suggestibility from the leaders.

A third group of bystanders actively intervenes to help the victim, and like face-to-face bullying, they can be a powerful force in either encouraging or stopping the bullying. However, unlike face-to-face bullying the bystander has far less opportunity to intervene as their role in cyber-bullying is often as a passive consumer of the malicious content. The bystander audience to cyber-bullying is usually far greater and far more dispersed and they often have little at their disposal to limit the harm done.

The New Workplace

To understand this new dimension of bullying it is important to understand how cyber technologies pervade our lives. Nowhere is this more apparent than in the lives of young people who have grown up with these technologies and are now entering the workforce. Recent university graduates entering the workforce have grown up in a web 2.0 world which has revolutionized the way that people use and share information on the internet. With the defining feature of web 2.0 being is its participatory quality, wherein everyday users can easily post and distribute information on the internet, these computer users are content creators. The added dimension of mobile devices provides an unlimited anytime, anywhere ability for these content creators.

When we say content creators, we are talking about every college or university student who has created a blog, posted something online, helped build a website, created an online profile, or uploaded photos and/or videos to a website. That is virtually everyone who has entered the workplace in the last ten years. For them the internet is a place for expression, to socialize, to play out their identities, and gather up the raw material they use for their creations.

For people marinated in this online world, it is not uncommon for them to use three or more forms of technology simultaneously. They can be instant messaging someone, host a three way video call on their mobile phone, and compose an email while looking up a reference on Google and listening to a podcast. The important thing is that for many people, this is not work, but part of their lifestyle. For people who were raised on it, using these technologies is like breathing.

This is a generation that has grown up in a broadcast environment using phone cameras and video to capture and then post content instantaneously. Content that can be damaging to others and to businesses. This generation has also grown up in a peer rating environment, ranking everything from their classmates' physical appearances to their teachers grading practices. The commentary that accompanies these rankings is almost always provocative, and controversial.

As noted above, this generation has grown up using these mediums and devices in ways that are deeply embedded in their lifestyle. With many of these same technologies are also employed in the workplace the boundary between work and "leisure" is blurred as they toggle back and forth between legitimate information sharing and gossiping. This blurry boundary can also confuse the employers expectations about the availability of workers outside the office and after hours, as workplace communications have become an anytime, anywhere, 24/7, inescapable occurrence.

Prevention

Employers may often assume that because many of their employees grew up in a high-tech world that they will use online communications in courteous and professional manner, but such as assumption is false. Many young adults are self-taught, and are simply emulating what they have been exposed too. Accordingly there is a pressing need to make up for this deficit in learning. Although the internet and online communications have been incredibly empowering, it is no secret that these technologies are often abused, and the online world is a deeply alienating and cynical world. The nameless and faceless of this world has a dehumanizing affect which comes through in the tone and style of communications. There is even a name for it, called "flaming"—using racing and retaliatory language to enflame the recipient. Simply put, communicators in this realm often don't know how to disagree, and when they do, nothing constructive will come of it as enflaming remarks instantaneously erupt. (The secretaries fighting over a ham sandwich on the company intranet) In addition to an online culture, there are many cues in the wider culture that reinforce this type of communication. For example, US election campaigns, send a message that it is good practice to publicly malign and humiliate a rival.

The assumption that we know how to use these new communication paradigms has perpetuated a scenario where there is very little in the way of best practices for communication. Many younger people have great difficulty properly communicating in traditional ways and would be hard pressed to compose a proper business letter. Literacy rates among people are in decline as they evolve new media literacies. What is being lost is not only the ability to construct proper sentences, but the ability to correspond in a professional and courteous manner. Training and education in best practices for these online communications is an essential step toward regaining decency in communicating that will provide for constructive debate and disagreement. Without it, workplace discourse and communication will be slowly eroded to a point where constructive disagreement, debate, dignity, and common decency have gone the way of quill pens.

Policies and Procedures

Computer policies can be designed to prohibit the improper use of workplace computing resources. Whatever policies and procedures exist, when a bully acts, the bad conduct should be addressed as quickly as possible, because an early response can prevent the situation from escalating.

For situations in which the employer or manager is the perpetrator, workplaces should ensure that workplace policies are clearly written to ensure support and protection for the target, with a grievance procedure that will permit the victim and workplace to stop bullying conduct before it proceeds too far.

Support the Victims

An essential practice for properly implementing policies and procedures is ensuring that there is support for the victim. Many victims avoid reporting bullies because they are embarrassed, fear being stigmatized, and believe the bully will retaliate. Similarly, people who observe bullying often will not report it for fear they will be the next target. Therefore, organizations should encourage victims and bystanders to report any online bullying conduct, and to the extent possible, promise anonymity and amnesty to those who report the problem.

Employers should believe victims. Of course, it is possible for a "victim" to falsely accuse another employee of bullying. Thus, the best practice is to take reports of bullying seriously and to investigate the situation as quickly and as thoroughly as possible.

The Law

It is worth reminding employees that some forms of cyber-bullying can constitute crimes, torts, or statutory violations. For example, in the United States, seventeen states have enacted legislation that prohibits bullying in the K-12 setting. Moreover, when the bully targets individuals in protected groups, it may constitute sexual or racial harassment. Depending on the content of the messages, the bully may be liable in tort for defamation, public disclosure of private facts, invasion of privacy, assault, or intentional infliction of emotional distress. He or she also may be subject to federal or state laws concerning telecommunications, online harassment, terrorist threats, or stalking.

Free Speech

Free speech and the internet raise some important questions for employees, employers, and managers. Until recently, there was little law governing what was and wasn't acceptable speech on the Internet. In fact, the U.S. Supreme Court didn't issue a ruling on Internet speech until 1997. In that year, the Court returned a verdict in the case of Reno v. ACLU that helped clarify how internet speech should be treated in the future. Although this decision applies to schools, the issues closely parallel the workplace, and there is likelihood that this jurisprudence could be applied to the workplace.

Although case law is still evolving in this area employers should consider the following questions before attempting to regulate employee internet use.

Was the content created as part of workplace tasks, such as the company email or intranet, if so, then the speech in question is considered employer sponsored and the employer is granted greater leeway in regulating speech that might be perceived to carry the endorsement of the organization.

If the content was created on a workplace computer during the employees free time might be trickier, the employee will likely contend the Tinker standard governs. Under that standard, the speech in question is entitled to protection under the First Amendment as long as it does not (a) cause a material or substantial disruption to the organization, or (b) infringe on the rights of others. An attorney for the organization, however, would likely argue that the speech should be held to the Hazelwood standard of expression because the organizations computers were being used.

These factors, of course, relate to the employees speech on the Internet that occurs on the company grounds. If the speech in question occurs on a private Web site, a different set of issues is at stake. Although case law is still evolving in this area, company officials should exercise caution before attempting to limit employee expression on a private Web site maintained off the organizations grounds. On one hand, organizations have a vital interest in keeping all members of their community safe; if an employee produces speech that constitutes a "true threat" or invades the rights of others, companies have a responsibility to act. However, in the majority of lawsuits between employees and employers so far, judges have been more likely to defend the free expression rights of the employee, whose speech they usually determined did not constitute a "true threat".

Because the Supreme Court has granted cyber-speech the highest degree of protection under the First Amendment, company officials need to be aware that employee speech that occurs off company grounds is private and not subject to the authority of the organization unless sit causes a substantial disruption. If, however, an employee's speech crosses the line and suggests actual physical harm—such as Eric Harris's Internet "hit list" prior to the Columbine massacre—then organizations should immediately consult an attorney.

Conducting a Workplace Assessment: Determining "At Risk" Position

© Susan Shaw & Andrew Faas, Iceberg Navigation, 2011. Used with permission.

The recent collapse of the 168 year old News of the World and the public humiliation of media mogul Rupert Murdoch should give rise to organizational leaders satisfying themselves that their cultures do not put their organizations at risk.

Murdoch's testimony before the British parliamentary committee was in essence an admission that he is totally out of the loop on how his organizations operate. For someone who has long had the reputation of being a hands on manager, his defense comes across as suspect. While we suspect that Murdoch may have been aware of some of the tactics to get the scoops scored by his newspapers, it is entirely possible that he did not fully understand or appreciate how a culture of fear can destroy an organization and it's people. Murdoch places the blame on those he trusted, he and his board should at the very least acknowledge management neglect.

It is our assertion that most organizational leaders do not fully understand or appreciate the power, both positive and negative, of organizational culture.

Many organizational leaders relegate the "cultural stuff" to their human resource people, believing that it is sufficient to have values and operating principles plastered all over the place, rarely assessing whether they are constantly applied and are reflective in the actual culture that exists.

We have found that it usually takes a major incident for organizational leaders to consider bullying as a major risk. In all of the instances where we were called in after a major incident, leaders in the organization were shocked to find that the incident could have been prevented had they paid closer attention to telltale sign that were evident. They were also amazed at how little they really knew about what was going on in their organization.

We encourage organizational leaders to be proactive in identifying the telltale signs and really understand the cultures that they lead and the impacts and risks involved.

We help organizations go through this process.

At Iceberg Navigation, we define culture as the way an organization operates, in everything it does.

To determine the actual culture that exists within an organization requires a comprehensive review of a number of fronts. As all of the fronts are interrelated, reviewing and analyzing them in isolation will not show the whole picture. Connecting this analysis with cultural indicators will yield insights that should capture the attention of even the most hardened and skeptical leader.

In assessing organizational cultures, Iceberg Navigation goes below the water line, helping organizations gain information that is not being brought forward. We look for undisclosed workplace cultural issues and connect seemingly unrelated events, comments and situations to identify the risks and opportunities.

Our experts have designed a comprehensive five stage assessment process that can be customized based on individual organizational needs.

The five stages are as follows:

Stage 1
Documentation and Program Review

We review and assess the effectiveness of the organizations:

- Policies and procedures
- Definition of workplace bullying and violence
- Employee surveys and their robustness
- Employee complaints
- Past incidence reports
- Employment programs
- Incident investigations

Stage 2
Analyzing the Fronts

This stage involves gaining a comprehensive interview-based understanding of the workplace. Employees at various levels are interviewed with assurances of confidentiality to determine workplace dynamics and the strengths and weaknesses of the organizational structure. This is where we delve into the eleven fronts:

- Governance
- Structure
- Decision making
- Politics
- Systems and technology

- Communication
- Roles and responsibilities
- Accountabilities
- Measurements
- Rewards and recognition
- Alignment

Stage 3

Cultural Indicators

A review and analysis of a number of cultural indicators will help identify the impacts that culture has on the individual and the organization. The indicators are:

- Staff turnover—overall organization—by department—by employee category.
- Run rate vacancies by department—by employee category.
- Absentee rate, short and long term—by department—by employee category.
- Stress leave experience.
- Frequency and severity of workplace accidents.
- History of suicides or attempted suicide.
- Participation rate of people using a employee assistance program EAP.
- Proportion of internal promotions to external hires for positions beyond entry level.
- Termination rate (i.e. those who are fired)—overall organization—by department.
- Resignation rate—overall organization—by department.
- Reasons people cite for leaving.

- History of grievances or complaints.
- History of human rights claims filed.
- Activity on whistleblower hot line or other vehicles used to report wrongdoings.

Stage 4
Survey Tool

The Survey Tool is used to identify the strength and weaknesses of organizational culture and provide an outlet for anonymity regarding harassment, bullying and violence.

Stage 5
Report and Recommendations

In our final stage, we present the outcome of the assessment process:

- Workplace Violence/Harassment Compliance Report.
- Identification of risk behaviors in the organization.
- A fear factor gauge.
- Report on the impact of existing systems, processes and practices.
- Recommendations for creating a sustainable, integrated anti bullying program.
- Baseline from which to annually measure improvement.

Benefits of conducting a comprehensive workplace assessment:

1. Provides senior management with the organizations risk profile.
2. Determines the prevalence of incidences and a baseline from which to track trending of risk profile.

3. Identifies areas of highest risk within the overall organization which assists in prioritizing changes and interventions.
4. Satisfy's legislative compliance requirements.
5. Provides a unique insight in what is really going on in an organization.

Whether an organization resembles a large public enterprise such as Murdoch's News of the World or a small, privately run manufacturing or consulting concern, its' leaders require an appreciation of the risks created from workplace culture. The damages arising to individuals, brand, and, indeed, enterprise, from a culture of intimidation, fear and bullying is as significant to an organization's well-being as those risks reviewed regularly by corporate accountants, lawyers and risk managers. We believe that a responsible board of directors and/or executive management team will benefit enormously from the heightened awareness of culture that the Iceberg Navigation assessment process reveals. Where an organization's culture and operational systems are positive, transparent and predictable, its employees, customers and shareholders will reward it with positive activities of their own.

Bullying and Performance Management

© David Poirier & Andrew Faas, Iceberg Navigation, 2011. Used with permission

Making Weak Management Strong

Ambiguity and subjectivity in performance management gives managers a license to bully and discredit their subordinates.

A host of European studies have found that many of the environmental characteristics that contribute to bullying are actually describing the functional features of a work unit and that most of them are also factors related to leadership style and supervisory practices. Heinz Leymann commented in his article, "The Content and Development of Mobbing at Work," "that of the eight hundred cases studied where mobbing (bullying) occurred frequently, an almost stereotypical pattern of poorly organized working methods and weak management were found."

Forcing people out of an organization is the number one motivation that bullies have for targeting their victims. Bullies usually use poor performance and/or a poor attitude to build a case against their target.

Without clear, fair, reasonable and measurable expectations, managers are left to their own devices to manage performance. Where there is a lack of systems to set and measure expectations, there is usually frustration.

Employees are frustrated because they are not sure of what is expected of them or feel they are being taken advantage of if the manager sets unrealistic targets, or uses favoritism in the allocation of work or, uses the lack of a system to set the employee up to fail. This frustration also causes employees attitude to sour.

When this happens, the bystanders or coworkers get frustrated. They are frustrated because they believe or are conditioned to believe that someone is not pulling their weight and if there is a poor attitude they are considered to be a complainer and/or a trouble maker. Where the target falls into "*a trap,*" the bystanders or coworkers usually side with the bully because the bully has proven that his target is a poor performer and/or has a bad attitude.

Without some form of performance management system in place, poor quality managers will become frustrated as well and lashes out at people who they believe are not meeting expectations.

Generally, employees at all levels respond well to clear expectations and enjoy working in high performance organizations. Being part of a winning team is a real motivator. The key to employees accepting, even embracing clear and high expectations is that they be fair and attainable and be measured. Predator bullies however, resist performance management systems and attempt to manipulate them.

There are various types of systems, including engineered labor standards. It largely depends on the type of operation and nature of work, which type of system is most effective. Most organizations have industry or sector benchmarks, best practice performance management systems, standards and targets available to them.

There is a myth that bullying legislation and/or anti-bullying policies restrict and limit managers from having open and honest conversations with their subordinates and that employees will abuse legislation and policies as a shield or a sword when they are challenged on performance or attitude issues. The reality is without performance management systems in place, organizations are at risk of having employees use legislation and/or policies to lodge complaints that they are being bullied, when they are challenged on performance. The other reality is, where there is a effective and fair performance management system in place there are fewer complaints, regardless of legislation or policies that are in place.

Research suggests that overloaded and bullied employees tend to work for organizations that are declining or shrinking, where the management style is bureaucratic and reactive. In contrast, those employees who feel purposeful, energized and recognized are those that work for growing, dynamic companies where the management style is empowering and successful.

With an effective and fair performance management system in place managers are able to have a positive discussion with their subordinates even when correcting deficiencies. Rather than lashing out, they are able to have a fact based conversation which addresses what the employee needs to do to meet expectations or targets and how the manager can help them vs threatening them.

Whistleblower Protection: Creeping Towards a Solution

© Richard Alderson, B.A., LL.B, Iceberg Navigation, 2011. Used with permission.

According to over ten thousand cases from the UK National Workplace Advice Line and cases reported through its web site, BULLY ONLINE, the 4th reason for being bullied is: "blowing the whistle on malpractice, fraud, illegality, breaches of rules, regulations and procedures, or raising health and safety issues". Such a high incidence of bullying in the context of the workplace leads to a number of important questions. What protections are there for whistleblowers when they decide to speak out about wrongdoing? Would the existence of more legislated protections encourage people to report wrongdoing or act as a deterrent to employers, even fellow employees, from retaliating against whistleblowers or promote greater compliance with laws and good ethical practices? Should organizations support reporting of wrongdoing within their organizations?

Introduction

A whistleblower can generally be defined as:

Someone who reports alleged mismanagement or illegal or corrupt or dangerous activities or some other wrongdoing about some activity they believe to be harmful to a public or private interest, occurring in a public or private business or in government.

It includes disclosure to other people within the organization, to outside regulatory bodies or law enforcement agencies or to the media.

Most of the high profile cases reported in the media involve people who speak out about issues involving public safety. Two examples readily come to mind:

1. Dr. Nancy Olivieri who spoke out regarding her concerns about the effects of a drug being used in a clinical trial on patients at the Hospital for Sick Children in Toronto, Ontario;
2. Anne Mitchell, a registered nurse who reported a physician to the Texas Medical Board for what she believed was unsafe patient care.

In the more common and less sensational cases, however, organizations are faced with employees who try to report wrongdoing by a coworker—frequently a superior, often involving any number of behaviours such as: violation of a criminal or regulatory law, financial misreporting, theft of company property, or violations of the company's business ethics policy. More often than not, however, without some protection most people will just keep their head down and not report anything, fearful of speaking out against behaviour of a superior who may be perceived as having the unquestioned support of more senior management within the organization.

Nevertheless, when a whistleblower does report what they believe to be wrongdoing, they make the report out of a sense of duty or obligation to do so. A whistleblower usually has nothing personal to gain by speaking out—contrary to allegations often made. In addition to feeling that speaking out is the right thing to do, a whistleblower perhaps realizes that by not speaking out they may be perceived to be complicit in the organization's wrongdoing.

A whistleblower usually goes through a period of struggle between their sense of loyalty to their organization and its leaders and with their sense of doing what is right. Depending on the circumstances, it is not uncommon for whistleblowers to undergo a further struggle: a struggle with their coworkers and employer which can result in their being ostracized by their coworkers, discriminated against by future potential employers, or even fired from their organization. This marginalization campaign is directed at whistleblowers with the goal of eliminating them from the organization. Such marginalization can be seen as a type of mob behaviour where even bystanders who are unaware of all the facts join in on the attacks based on misinformation that has been put about by people in a position of authority. Although this is an extreme form of workplace bullying wherein a group of people targets an individual, it is not uncommon.

Statutory Protection

Currently, protection for whistleblowers in Canada is narrow and is generally concentrated in the area of environmental, labor, employment standards and occupational health and safety law.

In the United States legislation at the federal level protects public-sector workers and in some states protection is afforded to both public and private sector workers. The greater development of whistleblower protection may be due to the legal concept of "employment at will" where dismissal for whistle blowing is seen as an exception to the employer's right to dismiss without notice. However, as we will see below, the American whistleblower experience is not necessarily better than their counterpart's in Canada.

Despite the shortcomings in the protections for whistleblowers in Canada and the United States, the protections there far exceed protections afforded whistleblowers in Europe.

The only country with all encompassing national whistleblower protection is the United Kingdom. The Public Interest Disclosure Act 1998 ("PIDA") applies to both public and public sectors, including agency staff, home workers, trainees, contractors and all professionals in the National Health Service (NHS). Generally, the only workers who are not protected are those who are genuinely self employed, volunteers, police officers and those ordinarily working outside Briton, and those in the armed forces or in the security or intelligence services.

Non-Statutory Protection

In addition to statutory protections, public and private sector employees who decide to become whistleblowers can seek protection under the common law. An employee owes their employer certain duties, chief among them being the duties of loyalty, good faith and, in some situations, confidentiality. The duty of loyalty means that the employee is required to perform their work assignments with diligence and skill, to be truthful on the job, to avoid conflicts of interest with their employer's interests, and to behave at all times in a manner that will not harm their employer's reputation.

Good faith by an employee requires performance of work assignments for the best interests of the employer who is paying the employee's wage or salary. The duty of confidentiality requires that an employee keep certain information confidential until such information is no longer confidential. In other words, until such time as the information has become stale or has become distributed beyond a recognized set of people, or has been expressly released by the employer. The duty can be contractual, or equitable, being recognized by a court whenever the employer entrusts an employee with "confidential" information on the understanding that it is not to be disclosed without authorization. A general duty of confidentiality may also be created by a particular relationship between the employer and the employee, for example as required by the position held by the employee in the organization whether defined by its seniority within the organization or its access to information understood to be confidential.

When an employee decides to become a whistleblower and releases confidential information, believing that to do so is in the public interest, the employee breaches these duties. The employer usually reacts by disciplining the employee, which can include dismissal from employment. Some employees have sought protection from the courts as part of a wrongful dismissal action.

When the disclosed wrongdoing has been serious and the public's interest in disclosure is clear, courts have permitted a very narrow public interest defence and have required the employee to first exhaust internal processes and procedures within the organization, to ensure the accuracy of the information disclosed, and to act reasonably in any given set of circumstances. Thus, absent express statutory protection or common law development, an employee currently has little protection under the common law and may seriously harm their livelihoods by deciding to join the ranks of whistleblowers.

Case Studies

There have been several incidences that have been widely reported over the past few years that show that organizations have a poor record in responding to whistleblowers and that whistleblower protection is full of pitfalls for the whistleblower. These cases also reveal two other significant points:

1. Even major, well respected institutions can show less than stellar responses to issues raised by their employees;
2. Even where there is seemingly adequate legislated protection for the whistleblower, gaps in such protection can be hazardous for the whistleblower. The following

cases, drawn from events in Canada and the United States, provide ample proof of the difficulties whistleblowers face.

Ouimet and the Office Of Integrity Commissioner

The first case involves the office of the first federal Public Sector Integrity Commissioner, Christiane Ouimet, previously mentioned. This case is not so much about a whistleblower, but about a legislated office failing to assist those (i.e. whistleblowers) for whom it was created. The Public Sector Integrity Commissioner is responsible for the administration of the federal Public Servants Disclosure Protection Act, which establishes a procedure for the disclosure of wrongdoings in the public sector, including the protection of whistleblowers who disclose wrongdoing.

Ms. Ouimet took office in August 2007. In October 2010 it was announced that the Office of the Public Sector Integrity Commissioner was being investigated by the office of the Auditor General of Canada. Shortly thereafter it was announced that Ms. Ouimet was leaving her position as Public Sector Integrity Commissioner. The Auditor General of Canada, Sheila Fraser, issued a scathing report in December 2010, slamming Ouimet for failing to fulfill her mandate and for berating and bullying her own staff. The Auditor-General's report found that, out of 228 complaints brought to the attention of the Integrity Commissioner's Office in the three years that Ms. Ouimet headed the office, only seven were investigated, and five of those were dismissed. No findings of wrongdoing were issued. Ironically, the report also described a hostile work environment fostered by an allegedly vindictive Ms. Ouimet, who in one instance apparently amassed binders full of information on a staffer whom she did not like. It was reported that eighteen of twenty-two staff members in one year had left and been replaced, a situation that Ms. Ouimet later described as due to a few discontented employees.

In a delayed appearance before the House of Commons' Public Accounts Committee, Ms. Ouimet responded, under oath, to the Auditor General's report by saying that she was shocked and appalled by the Auditor General's report and the subsequent fall-out. Ms. Ouimet stated that all complaints rejected by the Commission fell outside the mandate of her office, that she investigated employees because she had been advised on the potential for dangerous leaks and that staff members who griped about her were bitter about not getting promoted and had never supported her. Ms. Ouimet stated that she has always been known to do what is fair and what is right. Ms. Ouimet said that there were serious flaws and erroneous facts in the Auditor General's report that have attacked her reputation. Despite Ms. Ouimet's comments (or perhaps as evidenced by her comments) it is unlikely that it will ever be known truly why did Ms. Ouimet, the first ever integrity commissioner to be appointed, felt it was appropriate to investigate only 2 percent of the complaints filed with the office?

Of those who did file a report with the Integrity Commissioner's Office, at least two people felt ignored. One of these was Mr. Bruyea, a former intelligence officer turned veterans advocate, whose confidential medical files were circulated between hundreds of bureaucrats in an attempt to discredit him in his fight for better compensation for disabled soldiers. He sought out Ms. Ouimet's help on August 16, 2009. In a letter signed by Ms. Ouimet, the Integrity Commissioner's Office declined to take on his case, stating that none of the information he provided supported his claim of wrongdoing. According to Mr. Bruyea, after he made his disclosure to the Integrity Commissioner's Office, no one followed up with him for more information. Mr. Bruyea gained some vindication when Privacy Commissioner Jennifer Stoddart later ruled in

Mr. Bruyea's favour and a settlement was worked out with the government agreeing to pay Mr. Bruyea $400,000.

Another person was Hugh Danford, a former pilot and retired civil aviation inspector for Transport Canada. Following a 1999 crash in Davis Inlet which killed twenty-two year old Damien Hancock, Mr. Danford prepared a report documenting Transport Canada management's failure to act against the pilot of that plane. That pilot had already crashed four times and had a long history of other violations. The report also noted that Transport Canada was not implementing a Transportation Safety Board recommendation and that Transport Canada was negligent and partly responsible for the death of Damien Hancock. As punishment for speaking out persistently, Transport Canada senior management allegedly implemented a concerted effort to represent Mr. Danford as mentally unstable and insubordinate. At one point, Transport Canada management initiated information resulting in the arrest of Mr. Danford on unfounded allegations that he had made a death threat. The charges were dropped shortly thereafter, but the point had been made to Mr. Danford and other employees of Transport Canada. Ultimately, Mr. Danford left Transport Canada. In August 2008, Mr. Danford wrote to Ms. Ouimet making her aware of the miscarriage of justice by Transport Canada in the death of Damien Samuel Hancock and of the reprisals taken against him as a result of being a whistleblower. He received no satisfactory response from Ms. Oiument's office. Instead he felt he was intimidated during an interview by one of her investigators. Mr. Danford said that becoming a whistleblower destroyed his life and he received no help at all from the integrity commissioner's office.

The Commissioner is appointed by Parliament and is accountable to Parliament. However, the independence of the office was called into question after it was learned that there was a spate of emails between the Privy Council Office—Cabinet Office, ("PCO") and the Integrity Commissioner's Office and the involvement of the PCO in the settling of the severance package given to Ms. Ouimet although both she and the government have stated that Ms. Ouimet left her position voluntarily. Since many of the complaints filed with this office involved misuse of public funds and government assets, it would be highly-embarrassing to a government for these to be publicized. So the question is how can someone in this position properly perform a job when doing so might risk that very employment? Especially when government has traditionally not demonstrated dedication to allowing such agencies to operate unencumbered—and rewards those who keep their silence with generous severance packages? This issue extends to all watchdog agencies, whose loyalties would appear to be in conflict between their mandate and self-interest.

Olivieri and the Hospital For Sick Children

Another highly reported case involved Dr. Nancy Olivieri and the Hospital for Sick Children ("HSC") which is affiliated with the University of Toronto. Both the HSC and the University are well respected, major institutions in Canada. While working at the HSC, Dr. Olivieri entered into an agreement to test a new drug on behalf of Apotex, a large pharmaceutical company known primarily for its manufacture of generic drugs. When Dr. Olivieri discovered that some of her child patients involved in the test subjects were experiencing high levels of iron toxicity that could lead to life-threatening liver cirrhosis, Dr. Olivieri immediately stopped the tests and insisted that the health risks be communicated to her patients' parents. Apotex refused to agree to the release of any information, citing the agreement's non-disclosure clause. Apotex halted all further drug trials at the HSC, confiscated the trial medicine, terminated the test agreement with Dr. Olivieri thereby removing her from the study, and threatened her with legal action if she divulged any information to her patients or their parents.

Despite these actions by Apotex, Dr. Olivieri felt she had a duty to advise her patients' parents of the risks. Dr. Olivieri thought that the University and the Hospital would support her. She was wrong. Dr. Olivieri began receiving anonymous threatening letters from a coworker who was receiving Apotex funding for another study. Anonymous letters containing unfounded allegations against Dr. Olivieri were also sent to the media and the HSC disciplinary committee. Apotex, as well as some Hospital and University administrators, used these allegations to level charges against Dr. Olivieri and discredit her work. Six years after the first signs of problems with the drug were detected, the Independent Committee of Inquiry exonerated Dr. Olivieri of all allegations of misconduct. The Committee's report recommended that universities be prohibited from entering into research contracts that restrict the communication of results. The Committee was explicitly critical of the University and the HSC for failing to protect Olivieri's academic freedom. Subsequently news became known that at the time Dr. Olivieri came under attack, the University was in negotiations with Apotex over a $20 million building investment.

Mitchell and Winkler County Memorial Hospital

Staying with the medical theme, another case—from the United States, that garnered a lot of attention due to the fact that the whistleblower actually faced criminal charges as a result of her disclosures through an anonymous letter to state licensing board, involved Anne Mitchell who was a Registered Nurse at the Winkler County Memorial Hospital in Texas. A second nurse, Vickilyn Galle, who assisted Ms. Mitchell in writing the letter, was also charged but the charges were dropped prior to trial by the prosecutor's office. Ms. Mitchell, a highly trained nurse with twenty-five years experience, sent an anonymous letter to the

Texas Medical Board to express concerns about the standard of care provided by a physician who practiced at Winkler County Memorial Hospital. She was subsequently indicted for misuse of official information, more particularly for allegedly having used her position to obtain and disseminate confidential information—patient file numbers, but not patient names—in a letter to the medical board with the intent of harming Dr. Rolando G. Arafiles Jr. The prosecutor argued that state law required that reports of misconduct be made in good faith, and that Ms. Mitchell had been waging a vendetta against Dr. Arafiles since his arrival at the hospital in April 2008. In addition, Ms. Mitchell was terminated from her employment at the Hospital. In this case, Ms. Mitchell was able to count on financial and emotional support from the Texas Nurses Association (TNA) and the American Nurses Association (ANA) to support her through the criminal trial and her civil action for illegal retaliation and civil rights and due process violations.

At the criminal trial, other nurses confirmed that Ms. Mitchell had good grounds to be concerned about the doctor's malpractice, and the hospital administration had not dealt sufficiently with complaints made internally and had not done enough to support a whistleblower who clearly raised serious and viable concerns about patient care. The jury in Andrews, Texas, subsequently acquitted Ms. Mitchell, finding that Ms. Mitchell did nothing wrong by sending the file numbers in, since Ms. Mitchell is a nurse. The jury found no evidence of bad faith on the part of Ms. Mitchell.

The TNA and ANA expressed grave concerns about the potential chilling effect that the firing and subsequent criminal indictment would have on nurses, causing them to think twice before reporting questionable medical practice. Given the critical, duty-bound role of nurses in acting as patient safety advocates in the health care system, the question is whether nurse whistleblowers should never be fired and/or criminally charged for reporting questionable medical care, unless there is clear evidence of bad faith on the part of the nurse and that the report is false? The main issue in this case was patient safety—were the concerns expressed by the nurse justified? It appears that the Hospital was over zealous in its desire to protect a doctor at the expense of a nurse and it failed to adequately investigate and respond to the internal complaints that were made by Ms. Mitchell and Ms. Galle prior to going to the medical board. The Hospital's behaviour in this matter is even odder when one learns that Ms. Mitchell and Ms. Galle had both worked as the Hospital's compliance and quality improvement officers just prior to the incident.

Ms. Mitchell indicated that she thought long and hard whether to write the letter and it was fear of the retaliation that she ultimately did suffer that caused her to send the letter anonymously. Ms. Mitchell felt that the case had stained her reputation and said it had drained her savings. While the charges were pending, she was unable to find work and she felt alienated from her community which had become polarized by the case. Ms. Mitchell expressed concerns about the irreparable harm the case has done to her career.

This case also had a number of people who reportedly were in conflict of interest situations and were unable to keep their personal feelings separate from their duty. When Dr. Arafiles learned of the anonymous complaint, he claimed to the Winkler County sheriff that he was being harassed. The sheriff, purportedly an admiring patient who credits the doctor with saving him after a heart attack, was able to identify the nurses from the report and he obtained a search warrant to seize the two nurses' work computers and found the letter.

As in many jurisdictions, Texas does have whistleblower laws providing remedies for individuals who are retaliated against for protected activities and they appear to be fairly comprehensive. Protection of patient advocacy, specifically reporting concerns about a practitioner's patient standard of care, is provided for under Texas laws which include the Nursing Practice Act (which prohibits any person from suspending or terminating the employment of, or otherwise disciplining or discriminating against, a person who reports, without malice, reasonable concerns about the standard of care being provided by a medical health care practitioner), the Medical Practice Act (which provides immunity for anyone reporting in good faith a physician to the Texas Medical Board (as in the case of Mitchell) and the Title 5 of the Texas Government Code covering open government, ethics and protection for reporting violations of law. In fact the Texas Medical Board expressly reported that Ms. Mitchell's reporting to it of her concerns were within the Board's mandate to review.

However, there appears to be nothing in Texas law prohibiting a local prosecutor from pursuing criminal action as the Winkler County District Attorney did in Mitchell's case. It could be argued that such action is an abuse of the exercise of the discretion given to a prosecutor. However, taking this issue out of the context of this case, it is unlikely that anyone could have foreseen the need to try to limit the discretion of local prosecutors in this way. If this possibility was foreseen, it may have been viewed that any impingement on a prosecutor's discretion is an undue interference in the working of the justice system and that checks and balances within the prosecutor's office would prevent abuses that may arise from conflict of interest situations. The criminal prosecution of a nurse for reporting a patient care concern to a government licensing body seems to be a deficiency in the protection of the whistleblower protection afforded in Texas. Ms. Mitchell was ultimately successful in her civil action against her employer and others, obtaining a large settlement, but this result did not eliminate the emotional scars left by the ordeal experienced by Ms. Mitchell following her letter to the Texas Medical Board.

Events subsequently vindicated the nurses. The Texas Department of State Health Services ultimately fined the Hospital for inadequately supervising Dr. Arafiles and for firing Mitchell and Galle. The Texas Medical Board charged Arafiles with witness intimidation in addition to improperly treating nine patients. A Winkler County grand jury subsequently indicted Arafiles, former Winkler County Memorial Hospital administrator Stan Wiley, the Winkler County Sheriff, and the County Attorney who brought the charges for retaliation and misuse of official information. Wiley pleaded guilty to abuse of official capacity and was sentenced to thirty days in jail. Wiley's plea agreement includes a pledge to cooperate with prosecution of the other three.

Enron

Another interesting area that has received a lot of press attention lately in the wake of the Enron scandal has been whistleblowers in the corporate accounting and securities sectors. We mentioned earlier that public companies have instituted whistleblower systems in response to legislative initiatives on both sides of the border. It is the United States that has led in this area, no doubt partly because of the sheer size of the US capital markets, but also partly because of more robust protection for the whistleblower generally seen in the U.S. These sectors are areas where whistleblowers seem to be better received by coworkers, the press and others. One can understand why whistle blowing that uncovers financial misreporting or other wrongdoing that misleads shareholders would be welcomed as another way to ensure the integrity of capital markets and a country's financial system. However, it makes it all the more difficult to understand why similar welcoming arms are not extended to whistleblowers in other areas such as health care where patient safety should be paramount.

We have all read, or been exposed to, countless stories about the collapse of Enron Corporation ("Enron"). Many of the reports centered on the role played by Sherron Watkins who was Enron's vice president of corporate development. Ms. Watkins wrote an internal memorandum to her boss, Mr. Kenneth Lay, warning him about certain partnerships that Enron was involved in and the accounting for those partnerships and the risk to Enron. Her concerns were also expressed to Enron's auditors.

Ms. Watkins' memorandum was explicit and set out details of her concerns that Enron was more or less a Ponzi scheme. She indicated that she was incredibly nervous that Enron would implode in a wave of accounting scandals and that eight years of Enron work history would be worth nothing on her resume and that the business world would consider the past successes as nothing but an elaborate accounting hoax. Accounting for the failed partnerships, she wrote, was "a bit like robbing the bank in one year and trying to pay it back two years later." Ms. Watkins believed that these practices were wrong. She questioned whether Enron had become too risky a place to work? Here was an employee whose motives for reporting the wrongdoing seems to be twofold: first, Ms. Watkins knew the accounting was misleading investors and she clearly did not want to be a part of that wrongdoing; second, she wanted to protect her own professional credibility with potential employers.

In this case it is hard to claim that Ms. Watkins was a whistleblower in the commonly understood sense that most people would understand as "going public". Ironically, in her memo, Ms. Watkins expressed concerns about the possibility of other employees going public with this information. Ms. Watkins reported wrongdoing through internal reporting systems to her boss, who was the CEO. Her reporting memo was only made public through disclosure by congressional investigators.

Although Ms. Watkins' lawyer said there was no retaliation by colleagues at work when she returned to work following the release of her memo, Ms. Watkins reportedly was made to feel "an outcast." Some commentators have written that Ms. Watkins' memorandum was just another example in a long line of self-protection memos written by employees. These comments aside, Ms. Watkins seems to have done very well out of the Enron collapse, having gone on to build a successful business engaging in public speaking and consulting on whistle blowing. Nevertheless, the fact remains that Ms. Watkins had the courage to report to the top tier of management about serious matters and this should not be ignored. It could have ruined her career and she could have suffered some of the same personal attacks that other whistleblowers have suffered. It seems that a much more important line of inquiry should focus not on Ms. Watkins, but rather on two key questions: why did other Enron employees not come forward earlier? and if they had done so, could Enron have taken another path and avoided implosion?

In response to Enron and other corporate accounting scandals, the U.S Congress enacted An act to protect investors by improving the accuracy and reliability of corporate disclosures made pursuant to the securities laws, and for other purposes, commonly known as the Sarbanes—Oxley Act. In addition to requiring disclosure of all material off-balance sheet items, this Act directs the establishment of a set of internal procedures designed to ensure accurate financial disclosure. The signing officers must certify that they are "responsible for establishing and maintaining internal controls" and "have designed such internal controls to ensure that material information relating to the company and its consolidated subsidiaries is made known to such officers by others within those entities, particularly during the period in which the periodic reports are being prepared." The officers must "have evaluated the effectiveness of the company's internal controls as of a date within ninety days prior to the report" and "have presented in the report their conclusions about the effectiveness of their internal controls based on their evaluation as of that date."

External auditors are required to issue an opinion on whether effective internal control over financial reporting was maintained in all material respects by management. This is in addition to the financial statement opinion regarding the accuracy of the financial statements. The Sarbanes-Oxley Act requires the Audit Committee to establish procedures for the receipt, retention and treatment of complaints received by a company regarding accounting, internal accounting controls, or auditing matters, and the confidential, anonymous submission of concerns by employees regarding questionable accounting or auditing matters. It is envisioned that through these reporting systems, employees will be able to report their concerns on both a confidential and anonymous basis. The Act provides protection for whistleblowers who provide information about any fraudulent act by a public company to the Securities and Exchange Commission ("SEC") or during the course of an investigation relating to fraud against shareholders.

Very recently, the SEC decided to proceed with a whistle blowing policy that will allow the SEC to pay an award, subject to certain limitations, to eligible whistleblowers who voluntarily provide the Commission with original information about a violation of the federal securities laws that leads to the successful enforcement of a covered judicial or administrative action, or a related action. Retaliation by employers against individuals who provide the Commission with information about possible securities violations is strictly prohibited. The policy expressly allows employees to by-pass internal reporting systems and report direct to the Commission. This policy has drawn a lot of criticism by those who argued that SEC policy should require would-be corporate whistleblowers to use internal compliance rules, otherwise a company's existing compliance, legal, audit and similar internal reporting systems would be undermined.

Canadians may wonder whether rewarding people for reporting wrongdoing makes sense, however, the U.S. has decided it does as this legislation is not the first to reward whistleblowers.

In Ontario, Multilateral Instrument 52-110 of the Ontario Securities Commission ("OSC") incorporates some aspects of the whistle blowing process of the Sarbanes-Oxley Act. At the present time there are no corresponding protections for whistleblowers. However, the new head of the OSC has reportedly said that he would like the OSC to review the implementation of a whistleblower program.

Although these mandated systems may help those employees in public companies to report wrongdoing, they do not apply to private companies and they fall grossly short of what is required to protect whistleblowers properly. The Sarbanes-Oxley protections have proven thus far to be an expensive and time consuming remedy for employees. Even anonymous reports can be traced back to the reporter, as witnessed by the Mitchell case, and anonymous reports are notoriously vague. In Ontario there is no effective protection for people who want to report wrong doing in the corporate world.

Conclusion: Learning from the Cases

These cases illustrate how poor administrative decisions, provoked by conflicts of interest, can undermine an organization's handling of cases involving employees who report information about matters of important not only public interest, but public safety. The cases also demonstrate that even where legal protections exist, whistleblowers can get trapped in gaps in the protection provided by a number of statutory provisions. The medical cases are cogent because they involve issues that most people would readily see as high public interest—protecting people's lives. In the Olivieri case, there was a further public interest in supporting the free flow of information in the context of scientific research without which public safety is compromised as is the very nature of scientific enquiry. And yet public interests such as these have not proven to be significant enough to cause the people in authority to do the right thing. The most important issue in these cases is the threat to peoples' lives, not whether someone has breached a duty of confidentiality. If organizations had the appropriate culture which supported the proper internal systems for the reporting and investigation and resolution of wrongdoing or perceived wrongdoing, they would be better equipped to deal with these situations thereby saving not only lives, but also money and their reputations.

Many people argue that more legislation is required, but more is not necessarily best as the legislation currently in place seems to be more efficient in the creation of bloated bureaucracies than in the actual protection of individuals. From our short review above, we can see that an over-abundance of narrow focused legislation can be unproductive. The federal government's creation and passing of the Public Servants Disclosure Protection Act and its administration to date showcases how poorly our politicians can legislate when they want to and how ineffective the public bureaucracy can be. The Mitchell case illustrates how legislation can have gaps, whether intended or not. Undoubtedly any legislative response needs to be all encompassing, applying to both the public and private sectors and providing protection for whistleblowers who speak out in good faith to anyone about wrongdoing.

While we wait for government to get it right—to the degree it can, organizations should not sit on the sidelines. Clearly, leadership cannot, nor will not, come from government, so organizations—both public and private, have a unique opportunity to show both leadership and responsibility. Given the complexity of the situations which can arise in the workplace leading to legal liability or otherwise simply cause harm, organizations may benefit from developing and implementing adequate internal reporting systems. These reporting systems must not present a barrier to employees to report suspected wrongdoing. Indeed, appropriate internal channels must provide employees with confidence that reports made will be treated and acted upon in an appropriate manner by persons with authority. Learning that a problem exists within the organization allows the organization to determine whether it has the ability to deal with the matter internally. Third party involvement in the organization is minimized. Addressing issues when they are brought forward strengthens employee support for the organization and makes it less likely that such occurrences will occur because people know it will be reported and addressed.

Public companies and many private companies have implemented whistleblower programs to report financial wrongdoing in the wake of new financial reporting and governance initiatives that have occurred in recent years. These programs do not and are not intended to cover the reporting of non-financial wrongdoing. In fact, many companies discourage reporting of non-financial matters through their established whistleblower program because they are concerned about a tidal wave of frivolous complaints. However there is a cogent argument to be made that non-financial wrongdoing can do as much harm to a company as financial wrongdoing and it is surprising how often an investigation about a non-financial matter uncovers financial wrongdoing.

Wrongdoing such as discrimination, favouritism/nepotism, the violation of employment or environmental or other law, rule or regulation, mismanagement, gross waste of funds, abuse of authority, theft or misappropriation of company property, breaches of the company's business code of ethics, and activities that pose a substantial and specific danger to public health or safety can lead to substantial fines and damage to the reputation and credibility of a company. For example, where a company's import quality controls are ignored, the importation and distribution of a product hazardous to public health can result—as has happened with respect to imported candles, toy and earthenware products from China containing lead or other harmful substances. The costs of recalling the product, paying damages to injured customers and repairing the damage done to a company's reputation and credibility will be significant. Issues that are not addressed in an orderly and timely manner result in the expenditure of greater time and resources to address and resolve the issue at a later stage. It only makes sense that a company would want to know if someone is cutting corners on quality control systems and procedures. Programs do not have to be complicated and initial investigations arising from these programs can be done quickly. If the initial investigation does not resolve a report of wrongdoing then further appropriate investigation of those cases can be carried out.

There are many aspects that should form part an internal reporting system, whether for financial or non-financial wrongdoing. Some of these are:

1. There should be an independent reporting mechanism utilizing an external independent third party. This third party should communicate any reported wrong-doing to two different people in the organization.

2. The policy should state that information provided must be clear, truthful and made in good faith.

3. The policy should state clearly what "good faith" means. It doesn't mean that one is always right, just that one honestly thinks one is right or that one honestly thinks there is a valid issue that needs to be reviewed by someone with the skills and knowledge to do so.

4. The policy should ask for the who, what, when, where and why—who is involved, what action/non-action is it that the whistleblower thinks is wrong, where and when did the perceived wrong-doing occur, who witnessed the

behaviour, and why does the whistleblower think it is wrong. Supporting documentation should be requested. The request for such details will assist in the investigation and will help to discourage false, frivolous or bad faith claims.

5. Confidentiality is to be guaranteed. No attempt to discover the identity of a whistleblower should be made. The policy should encourage the giving of the whistleblower's name as it will make the investigation easier and more effective. If the name is given, then an assurance of non-disclosure of the name should be provided to the extent possible. It is fair for the policy to advise that failure to provide a name or details of the alleged wrongdoing may compromise the organization's ability to investigate.

6. A strict non-retaliation policy must be stated, adhered to and enforced. It is certainly arguable that if people "in the know" have sufficient protection against retaliation, certain situations would not have occurred.

7. All reported matters should be investigated.

8. If the whistleblower is known, then providing an update on the investigation may be useful, while making it clear that confidentiality may restrict the disclosure of details of the investigation to the whistleblower. The point is to address the concern of the whistleblower that something is being done to investigate the wrongdoing reported, otherwise the whistleblower may take their concerns to the media or another third party.

9. In reviewing reports, the analysis should proceed on the assumption that the report was made in good faith, unless there is clear evidence to rebut that assumption. Note that this does not mean that there is an assumption that the report is true, which must be determined based on the investigation.

10. Incorporate into your organization's culture the knowledge that wrongdoing will not be condoned and that everyone has a duty to report any suspected wrongdoing to a supervisor or through the organization's independent whistleblower program. Part of this process will be to ensure that the whistleblower program is publicized. One company took pride that there had never been a report under its whistleblower program only to learn that most employees were unaware of it.

11. Senior management support for the reporting of wrongdoing and the correction of proven wrongdoing has to be stated clearly and unequivocally and seen to be real in both word and deed.

Index

60 Minutes – 100
A Colossal Failure of Common Sense – 70, 304
A Silence That Hangs Over CEO's – 129, 306
A theory of cognitive dissonance – 44, 303
ABC News' - 179
Aggression Among University Employees – 149, 306
AIG – 38, 69, 70, 244
Alderson, Richard – 11, 147, 247, 267
Alfred University – 142, 306
Alice in Wonderland - 179
American Institute of Stress (AIS) - 173
Apotex – 275, 276
Arafiles, Rolando G. Jr, Dr. – 277, 278, 280
Archbishop - 227
Arkansas - 175
Armstrong, Lance – 99, 100, 101, 116
Ashland School District - 175
Asia - 170
Australia – 122, 123, 169, 170, 175, 305, 307
Bain Capital - 57
Barchi, Robert L. - 66
Beale, David – 103, 305
Bear Stearns – 38, 303
Bethesda, Maryland - 177
Bjorkqvist, Kaj – 149, 306
Bloomberg, Michael – 189, 305

Boards That Deliver – 69, 304
BP PLC - 129
British Columbia – 48, 50, 108, 158, 305
Brown - 50
Brown, John –129
Bruyea, Mr. – 273, 274
Bullied: a Student, a School, and a Case That Made History - 175
Burlington Northern vs White decision of the U.S. Supreme - 147
Court (2006)
California - 178
Camus, Albert - 118
Canada – 1, 15, 23, 39, 49, 50, 57, 61, 91, 92, 114,130, 157, 158,159, 160, 161, 243, 269, 272, 274, 275
Canada's GLBT magazine - 130
Canadian Broadcasting Service - 47
Cananni, Eli, Dr. - 13
Carlton University - 49
Cassano, Joe - 70
Catholic Church – 15, 54
CBC News – 50, 303
Center for Disease Control - 176
Chapman, Rose, PhD – 169, 307
Charan, Ram – 67, 69, 304
Charles Bank - 57
Ching, Cyrus - 211
Chitale, Radha - 179
Chrysler - 91
Churchill, Winston - 203
Cirocco, Virginia - 11
CNN - 130
Columbine - 256
Cooper, Anderson - 130
Crawford, Alison – 50, 303

Curtin University of Technology - 169
Danford, Hugh - 274
Daniels, Charles - 174
David, Jones – 123, 305
Davis inlet - 274
Davis, Nick – 303
de Becker, Gavin - 178
Detroit, MI - 170
Dignity at work Campaign – 99, 103
DLJ - 57
Dorner, Christopher - 176
Duncan, SM – 108, 305
Duxbury, Linda - 49
Educating to Eliminate – pg 139
Eichmann, Adolf - 45
Elliot, William - 50
Emerson, Ralph Waldo - 214
Enright, Michael – 176, 177
Enron – 38, 67, 187, 244, 280, 281, 282
Equity - 130
Ernst and Young - 38
Estabrooks, CA. – 108, 305
Europe – 148, 170, 179, 263, 269
European Journal of work and Organizational Psychology – 179, 307
Faas Foundation - 13
Faas, Catherine - 11
Facebook - 107
FBI - 130
Federal Express – 146
Fed Ex - 146
Fenner, Robert – 122, 305
Festinger, L. – 44, 303
Fortune 1000 - 129

France - 177
France Telecom – 177, 178
Fraser, Sheila – 39, 272, 303
Fraser-Kirk, Kristy – 122, 123
Frost, Robert - 223
Fuld, Richard - 70
Fuller, Thomas - 212
Galle, Vickilyn, RN – 276, 278, 280
Gandhi, Mahatma – 19, 241, 246
Gap Inc. - 1
Gavin de Becker & Associates, Inc - 178
German – 45, 179
Gleevec – 13
Good Boss, Bad Boss – 108, 305, 307
Grant, Jennifer - 11
Greenberg, Allen – 38, 303
Grimme, Sheryl and Don – 7, 303
Grove, Andy - 69
Gruson, Karen - 11
Guardian News Services - 39
Gustafsson, Annelie – 179, 307
Hamilton, Alexander - 150
Hancock, Damien - 274
Haney, John - 11
Haney, Velvet - 11
Harding, Tonya - 116
Hare, Robert – 197, 307
Harris, Eric - 256
Hazlitt, William - 106
Heat Group - 123
Hewlett Packard - 83
Hjelt-Back, Monika – 149, 306
Hoare, Sean – 39, 303
Hoel, Helge – 103, 305

Hooters - 141
Hoover, Nadine - 142
Hospital For Sick Children – 268, 275
Human Rights Campaign - 129
Hyndman, K. – 108, 305
Iceburg Navigation (IN) – 147, 247
Inside the Secret World of Ottawa and the RCMP – 48, 304
Intel - 69
International Communications Research – 148, 306
International Federation of Accountants (IFAC) – 68, 241, 304
International Labor Organization - 187
Is this the end of the Toxic Boss? - 49
Israel Cancer Research Fund (ICRF) - 13
Israeli Scientist - 13
Jackson, Ryan - 11
Jerusalem - 45
Jesuit Order - 54
Johnson, F. Ross - 1
Keaschly, Loraleigh - 170
Keller, Helen - 205
Kerrigan, Nancy - 116
KKR - 57
Korea's Defense Ministry - 176
Kwoh, Leslie – 129, 306
Labrosse, Catherine – 1, 11
Lackland Air Force Base - 123
Laney College - 179
LAPD – 163, 176
Lehmann Bothers - 244
Lepowsky, William - 179
Lewis, Michael – 70, 304
Leymann, Heinz, Dr. – 149, 179, 180, 263, 306, 307
Loblaw – 58, 91
Loblaw Companies Limited – 114

Lockheed Martin - 174
Lombard, Didier - 178
Long Walk to Freedom - 226
Lord of the Flies - 80
Louis Harris and Associates – 122, 305
McDonald, Lawrence G. – 70, 304
Mandela, Nelson - 226
Mattice, Catherine - 7
McCallion, Hazel - 140
McClelland, Susan - 11
McCutheon, Bob - 114
McInness, Mark – 122, 123
Mcleans Canada - 49
Mcluhan, Marshall - 111
Mean Girls - 80
Messick, Virginia - 123
Meyers, Robert - 142
Milgram Experiment - 45
Milner, Peter – 121
Ministry of Labor – 139, 140
Mississauga, Ontario – 139, 140, 141, 142, 306
Mitchell, Anne – 268, 276, 277, 278, 279, 280, 284, 285
MLB - 130
Mobbing at Work and the Development of Post Traumatic Stress - 307
Disorder
Morgan, Tony - 173
Morrissey, Kevin - 177
Mounties Under Fire - 47
Murdoch, Rupert – 39, 257, 262
Murphy, Glenn – 1, 58
Murray, Jane - 177
Muslim – 130, 177
Nabozay, Jamie - 175

Namie, Gary Dr. – 99, 119, 170, 305, 306, 307
Namie, Ruth, Dr. – 99, 170
National Center for Transgender Equality and the National Gay and Lesbian Task Force - 131
National Gallery of Victoria, Australia - 175
National Work Advice Line – 147, 306
Nazi – 45
NBA – 130
NBL - 130
Needham, Richard J - 105
New York (NY) – 170, 189
New York City – 167, 189
New Zealand - 170
News of the World – 39, 257, 262, 303
NFL - 130
Niemollers, Marten - 215
North Carolina - 175
Norwood, Brittany - 177
Nurses' Experience of Violence – 108, 305
O'Brien, Andrew - 175
Olivieri, Nancy, Dr. – 268, 275, 276, 284
Ontario – 1, 91, 92, 139, 243, 268, 284
Ontario Teachers' Pension Plan - 57
Ontario Transportation and Works Department 139, 140
Osterman, Karin - 149
Ouimet, Christine – 39, 272, 273, 274, 275, 303
Owning Up – 69, 304
Ozanam, Frederic - 97
Palango, Paul – 48, 304
Palm Beach - 117
Paulson, Bob - 50
Payton, Laura – 50, 303
Pearson, Christine – 173, 307
Peel Regional Police - 140

Pelly, Scott - 100
Pernette, Tim - 66
Petrecca, Laura - 303
Poirier, David – 11, 247, 263
Pope, Benedict - 54
Pope, Francis - 54
Pope, Eleanor - 11
Porath, Christine – 173, 307
Post Traumatic Stress Disorder (PTSD) – 16, 25, 48, 82, 179, 180, 181, 213, 307
Pound, Glenn – 11, 247, 249
Public Sector Integrity Commissioner – 39, 272, 303
RCMP Values-Driven Leadership - 48
Reinholdt, Bobbi - 11
Rice, Mike - 66
Rice, Robert - 39
RJR Nabisco - 1
Rodgers, Robbie - 130
Rollie – 9, 10
Rolling Stone magazine – 70, 304
Roosevelt, Eleanor - 207
Roosevelt, Theodore - 185
Rotman Commerce program - 1
Royal Canadian Mounted Police (RCMP) – 15, 46, 47, 48, 49, 50, 163
Russell, Jonathan - 178
Rutgers University – 66, 176
Saint Louis, France - 177
Scarlet Kings - 66
Schneider, Joe – 122, 305
Scott, Sara - 49
Sexual Respect Curriculum - 121
7 Issues facing the RCMP commissioner – 50, 303
Seneca - 148

Shaw, Susan – 11, 247, 257
Shoppers Drug Mart – 15, 57
Shore, Dinah - 206
Skilling, Jeffery - 187
Smith, Donald W. - 50
Solomon Lew's Premier Investments - 123
South Korea - 176
Southern Poverty Law Center – 130, 175, 306
Stanford, CA - 303
Stanford Prison Study - 44
Stanford University – 44, 303
Stoddart, Jennifer - 273
Stokowski, Laura A. – 107, 305
StopHazing.org - 139
Studio City – 178, 307
Sulz, Nancy – 50, 175
Superior Forestry Service, Inc. - 175
Sutton, Robert – 108, 305, 307
Tate Publishing – 6, 11
Tewksbury, Mark - 129
Texas Medical Board – 268, 277, 279, 280
Thavis, John - 54
The Business of Crime - 39
The Cost Of Bad Behavior: How Incivility is Damaging Your Business and What To Do About It - 173
The Gutenberg Galaxy - 111
The International Cycling Union (ICU) - 100
The Industrial Society - 173
The Perils of Obedience – 37, 46, 303
The Rise and Fall of Bear Stearns – 38, 303
The Vatican Diaries - 54
The Williams Institute – 130, 305, 306
Thurber, James - 214
Tiabbi, Matt – 70, 304

Tigart, Travis - 100
Time Magazine - 106
Toronto – 167, 268
Toronto Star – 140, 141, 142, 304
Transport Canada - 274
Tutu, Desmond - 227
Tyco - 67
US Anti-doping Agency (USADA) - 100
U.S. Equal Opportunity Commission - 148
United Kingdom - 270
United Nations - 177
United Nations Conference on Trade Development (UNCTAD) – 68, 241
United States – 6, 23, 61, 130, 147, 170, 174, 176, 249, 255, 269, 272, 276, 280
United States National Crime Prevention Council - 249
University of Southern California –173
University of Toronto – 1, 275
University of Virginia - 177
US (Postal Service) team - 100
US Department of Justice - 7
US Equal Employment Opportunity Commission (EEOC) – 122, 147
USA – 6, 173
USA Today - 303
US National Institute for Occupational Safety and Health - 176
Utica - 170
Vancouver – 158, 161
Vancouver Q Hall of Fame - 129
Vanity Fair – 70, 304
Violence: Not in My Job Description – 107, 305
Virginia Quarterly Review - 177
Vlahovic, Paris – 1, 11
Wall Street – 70, 304

Wall Street Journal – 129, 306
Watkins, Sharron – 38, 281, 282
Wayne State University - 170
Weimaraner - 9
Wells, Lee, John - 11
Wilde, Oscar - 35
Wilson, Woodrow - 208
Windsor, Ontario - 91
Winkler County Memorial Hospital – 276, 277, 280
Wisconsin - 175
Workplace Bullying Institute – 99, 119, 146, 170, 171, 307
WorldCom - 67
Yale University – 45, 46
Xtra - 130
Zaccerdelli, Giuliano – 47, 48
Zimbardo, Philip, Dr., PH.D - 44
Zogby International – 170, 171, 307
Zogby, John - 170

Endnotes

Grimme, Sheryl and Don. "'Violence in the Workplace - The Realities and the Options." *Business Know How*.

Petrecca, Laura. "Bullying by the boss is common but hard to fix." *USA Today*, December 28, 2010.

Part One

Bronskill, Jim, and Joan Bryden. "Ex-staffers bristle at Ouimet's 'Cadillac package'." *Canadian Press*, March 09, 2011.

Milgram, Stanley. Harper's Magazine. "The Perils of Obedience." *Abridged and adapted from Obedience to Authority*, 1974.

Payton, Laura and Crawford, Alison. "7 issues facing the RCMP commissioner." *CBC News*, October 27, 2011. http://www.cbc.ca/news/politics/story/2011/10/27/pol-list-rcmp-issues-comissioner.html.

Greenberg, Allan. *The Rise and Fall of Bear Stearns*. Simon & Schuster, 2010.

Fraser, Sheila. The Public Sector Integrity Commissioner of Canada - Report of the Auditor-General's, "Office of the Auditor General of Canada." December 14, 2010. http://www.oag-bvg.gc.ca

Davis, Nick. "Sean Hoare knew how destructive the News of the World could be." *The Guardian*, July 18, 2011.

The Diagnostic and Statistical Manual of Mental Disorders IV

Festinger, L., ed. Stanford, CA: Stanford University Press, 1957. s.v. "A theory of cognitive dissonance."

Skelton, Chad, and Andrea Woo. "More than 200 B.C. RCMP employees now on sick leave." *Vancouver Sun*, June 24, 2010.

Paul Palango, *Dispersing the Fog: Inside the Secret World of Ottawa and the RCMP*, (Key Porter Books, 2008), 255.

Skelton, Chad. "Six in 10 B.C. RCMP staff have thought about quitting." *Vancouver Sun*, May 12, 2010.

"RESTORING THE HONOR OF THE RCMP." *ADDRESSING PROBLEMS IN THE ADMINISTRATION OF THE RCMP'S PENSION AND INSURANCE PLANS.* (December 2007):39th Parliament, 2nd session, 11and 117.

MacCharles, Tonda. "Revolt in senior ranks spurs probe of RCMP chief." *toronto star*, July 28, 2010.

www.**rcmp**-grc.gc.ca/index-eng.htm

"Accountancy Summit on Corporate Governance Reform Looks Beyond the Global Financial Crisis." (Oct 2010). http://www.ifac.org/news-events/2010-10/accountancy-summit-corporate-governance-reform-looks-beyond-global-financial-cri.

Charan, Ram. *Owning Up.* Jossey-Bass, 2009.

Charan, Ram. *Boards That Deliver.* Jossey-Bass, 2005.

McDonald, Lawrence G. *A Colossal Failure of Common Sense.* Crown Business, 2010.

Lewis, Michael. "The Man Who Crashed the World." *Vanity Fair*, August 2009. http://www.vanityfair.com/politics/features/2009/08/aig200908

Tiabbi, Matt. "How Wall Street Is Using the Bailout to Stage a Revolution." *Rolling Stone magazine*, April 02, 2009. http://www.rollingstone.com/politics/news/how-wall-street-is-using-the-bailout-to-stage-a-revolution-20090402

Part Two

"The Dignity at work Compign," http://dignityatwork.org

Namie, Gary. "US Workplace Bullying Survey." (September 2007) WBI.

Namie, Gary. "(Still) Bullying With Impunity, Labor Day Survey." (September 2009), WBI.

Beale, David and Helge Hoel. "Workplace bullying, industrial relations and the challenge for management in Britain and Sweden." *European Journal of Industrial Relations* 16(2), 101—118;

Stokowski, Laura A. "Violence: Not in My Job Description." *Medscape*, August 23, 2010. http://www.medscape.com/viewarticle/727144.

Duncan, SM, K Hyndman, CA Estabrooks, and et al. "Nurses' experience of violence in Alberta and British Columbia hospitals." *National Library of Medicine (NLM)*. (2001): 32(4):57-78.. http://www.ncbi.nlm.nih.gov/pubmed/11928302.

Beckford, Martin. "Nine out of 10 say they are bullied at work." *The Telegraph*, November 06, 2008. http://www.telegraph.co.uk/news/uknews/3392320/Nine-out-of-10-say-they-are-bullied-at-work.html.

Sutton, Robert. *Good Boss, Bad Boss*. New York: Business Plus, 2010.

Louis Harris and Associates. workharassment.net, "Sexual Harassment in the Workplace." http://www.workharassment.net/index.php/sexual-harassment-in-the-workplace.html.

Fenner, Robert, and Joe Schneider. "David Jones, Ex-CEO McInnes, Sued by Publicist in Australia Federal Court." *Bloomberg.com*, August 02, 2010. http://www.bloomberg.com/news/2010-08-02/david-jones-former-chief-executive-sued-by-employee-for-sexual-harassment.html.

Burns, Crosby, and Jeff Krehely. The Williams Institute, "Gay and Transgender People Face High Rates of Workplace Discrimination and Harassment." 02 June, 2011. http://

williamsinstitute.law.ucla.edu/press/gay-and-transgender-people-face-high-rates-of-workplace-discrimination-and-harassment/.

Kwoh, Leslie. "A Silence That Hangs Over CEO's." *The Wall Street Journal*, July 25, 2012. http://online.wsj.com/article/SB10000872396390443295404577547043705374610.html

"Southern Poverty Law Center," http://www.splcenter.org/.

"The Williams Institute." http://williamsinstitute.law.ucla.edu/.

Grant, Jaime M., Lisa A. Mottet, and Justin Tanis. "Injustice at Every Turn." *A Report of the National Transgender Discrimination Survey.* (2011): 9.

McLean, Jesse, and David Rider. "Police probe duct-tape hazing at Mississauga workplace." *TheStar.com*, June 03, 2010.

Alfred University Study, April 2000, hazing

Turner, Heidi. "FedEx Age Discrimination." *LawyersandSettlements.com*. (February 11,2007). http://www.lawyersandsettlements.com/articles/employment/fedex-age-disrimination-00603.html.

Namie, Gary. "US Workplace Bullying Survey." (September 2007) WBI.

Namie, Gary. "How Employers and Co-workers Respond to Workplace Bullying." (Labor Day 2008), WBI.

UK and National Work Advice Line

"International Communications Research," http://www.icrsurvey.com/

Leymann, Heinz. "The Content and Development of Mobbing at Work." *European Journal of Work & Organizational Psychology*. 1996, 5 (2), 165-184.

Bjorkqvist, Kaj, Osterma, Karin, and Hjelt-Back, Monika. "Aggression Among University Employees." *Aggressive Behavior*. (1994): 173-184.

Chapman, Rose PhD, Curtin University of Technology in Perth, Australia, (2009)

"Workplace Bullying Institute," http://www.bullyingstatistics.org/content/workplace-bullying.html

Zogby International, http://www.zogby.com

Namie, Gary. "(Still) Bullying With Impunity, Labor Day Survey." (September 2009), WBI

Porath, Christine, and Christine Pearson. "How Toxic Colleagues Corrode Performance." *Harvard Business Review*, April 2009.

Porath, Christine, and Christine Pearson. *The Cost Of Bad Behavior.* 2009.

Kinder, Andrew and Cooper, Cary L The cost of suicide and sudden death within an organization (UK); Death Studies 33: 411-419, 2009.

Gavin de Becker Associates & Associates, Inc. Studio City, California

Robertson, Jordan. "California jury awards $61 million to two FedEx drivers in harassment lawsuit." *Associated Press*, June 3, 2006.

Leymann, Heinz and Annelie Gustafsson. "Mobbing at Work and the Development of Post Traumatic Stress Disorder." *European Journal of Work and Organizational Psychology*, 1996 5(2), 251-27)

Part Three

Robert Hare http://www.hare.org

Part Four

Fadiman, Clifton. *The American Treasury.* New York : Harper, 1955

Sutton, Robert. *Good Boss, Bad Boss.* New York: Business Plus, 2010.

Appendices

Blair, Julie. "New Breed of Bullies Torment Their Peers on the Internet." 22 *Education Week 6*, February 05, 2003. http://web4.epnet.com

Kabay, M.E. "Anonymity and Pseudonymity in Cyberspace: Deindividuation, Incivility and Lawlessness Versus Freedom and Privacy." *Ann. Conf. European Inst. For Computer Antivirus Research*. (1998).

(adapted from, Case Study: Cyber-bullying and Free Speech, the Knight Foundation)

Hasselback, Drew. "New OSC boss calls for new enforcement tools." *Financial Post*, February 23, 2011.

Canadian Environmental Protection Act, 1999, S.C. 1999, c.33

Canada Labour Code, R.S.C., 1985, c.L-2

Canadian Human Rights Act, R.S.C., 1985, c. H-6

Criminal Code, R.S.C., 1985, C.46

Public Servants Disclosure Protection Act, S.C. 2005, c. 46

For a more complete view of the short-comings of the PSDPA, see the website of the Federal Accountability Initiative for Reform; fairwhistleblower.ca

Environmental Protection Act, R.S.O. 1990, c. E.19

Environmental Bill of Rights 1993, S.O. 1993, c. 28

Occupational Health and Safety Act, R.S.O. 1990, c. O-1

Employment Standards Act 2000, S.O. 2000, c. 41

Public Service of Ontario Act, 2006, S.O. 2006, c. 35, Sched. A

Employment Standards Act, R.S.N.B. 1982, c. E - 7.2

Nursing Practice Act, Texas Occupations Code, Title 3, Subtitle E, Chapter 301

Medical Practice Act, Texas Occupations Code, Title 3, Subtitle B, Chapter 160

Texas Government Code, Title 5, Subtitle A, Chapter 554

Pub.L. 107-204, 116 Stat. 745

New OSC boss calls for new enforcement tools", by Drew Hasselback, Financial Post, February 23, 2011.

Public Interest Disclosure Act 1998, 1998 c.23

Five years of the Public Interest Disclosure Act in the UK: Are Whistleblowers Adequately Protected? David Lewis and Stephen Homewood, Centre for Legal Research, Middlesex University. http://webjcli.ncl.ac.uk/2004/issue5/dlewis5.html; Ten years of Public Interest Disclosure Legislation in the U.K.: Are Whistleblowers Adequately Protected?, David Lewis. *Journal of Business Ethics 82 (2):497 - 507.*

www.imf.org/external/hrd/integrity/index.htm

e|LIVE

listen|imagine|view|experience

AUDIO BOOK DOWNLOAD INCLUDED WITH THIS BOOK!

In your hands you hold a complete digital entertainment package. In addition to the paper version, you receive a free download of the audio version of this book. Simply use the code listed below when visiting our website. Once downloaded to your computer, you can listen to the book through your computer's speakers, burn it to an audio CD or save the file to your portable music device (such as Apple's popular iPod) and listen on the go!

How to get your free audio book digital download:

1. Visit www.tatepublishing.com and click on the elLIVE logo on the home page.
2. Enter the following coupon code:
   b5fa-0af3-fca5-7c21-5460-830b-cc61-4e41
3. Download the audio book from your elLIVE digital locker and begin enjoying your new digital entertainment package today!